Cultural Appropriation

Other Books of Related Interest

Opposing Viewpoints Series
Banned Books
The Future of Higher Education
The New Censorship

At Issue Series
Male Privilege
The Media's Influence on Society
Mob Rule or the Wisdom of the Crowd?

Current Controversies Series
Freedom of Speech on Campus
Hate Groups
Historical Revisionism

> "Congress shall make no law ... abridging the freedom of speech, or of the press."
>
> *First Amendment to the U.S. Constitution*

The basic foundation of our democracy is the First Amendment guarantee of freedom of expression. The Opposing Viewpoints series is dedicated to the concept of this basic freedom and the idea that it is more important to practice it than to enshrine it.

Cultural Appropriation

Gary Wiener, Book Editor

Published in 2024 by Greenhaven Publishing, LLC
2544 Clinton Street,
Buffalo NY 14224

Copyright © 2024 by Greenhaven Publishing, LLC

First Edition

All rights reserved. No part of this book may be reproduced in any form without permission in writing from the publisher, except by a reviewer.

Articles in Greenhaven Publishing anthologies are often edited for length to meet page requirements. In addition, original titles of these works are changed to clearly present the main thesis and to explicitly indicate the author's opinion. Every effort is made to ensure that Greenhaven Publishing accurately reflects the original intent of the authors. Every effort has been made to trace the owners of the copyrighted material.

Cover image: Kiselev Andrey Valerevich/Shutterstock.com

Library of Congress CataloginginPublication Data

Names: Wiener, Gary, editor.
Title: Cultural appropriation / edited by Gary Wiener.
Description: First edition. | New York : Greenhaven Publishing, 2024. | Series: Opposing viewpoints | Includes bibliographical references and index.
Identifiers: ISBN 9781534509634 (pbk.) | ISBN 9781534509641 (library bound)
Subjects: LCSH: Cultural appropriation--Juvenile literature. | Postcolonialism--Social aspects--Juvenile literature. | Acculturation--Juvenile literature.
Classification: LCC HM621.C76 2024 | DDC 306--dc23

Manufactured in the United States of America

Website: http://greenhavenpublishing.com

Contents

The Importance of Opposing Viewpoints	11
Introduction	14

Chapter 1: Is Cultural Appropriation Insult or Homage?

Chapter Preface	19
1. How Cultural Appropriation Is Defined *Encyclopædia Britannica*	22
2. Self-Appointed Gatekeepers of Culture Are Dangerous *Kenan Malik*	28
3. There Is a Fine Line Between Cultural Appropriation and Cultural Appreciation *Joshua E. Kane*	35
4. Context Is Everything When It Comes to Borrowing Culture *Andy Pratt*	40
5. Cultural Appropriation Is Cultural Cannibalism *Jennifer Whitney*	44
6. Cultural Appropriation Should Be Avoided *Copibec*	49
7. Cultural Appropriation Has Its Benefits *Steve Patterson*	54
Periodical and Internet Sources Bibliography	62

Chapter 2: Is Cultural Appropriation a Problem in the Music Industry?

Chapter Preface	65
1. Cultural Appropriation Is Widespread in the Music Industry *Parlé Magazine*	68

2. South African Band Die Antwoord's Success Is a Blatant Example of Cultural Appropriation   75
   Adam Haupt
3. Cultural Appropriation Has Been the Norm in Pop Music   81
   Rachel Martin
4. The Work of George Gershwin Shows that the Question of Cultural Appropriation in Music Is Not New   86
   Ryan Raul Bañagale

Periodical and Internet Sources Bibliography   91

Chapter 3: Is Cultural Appropriation a Problem in the Film Industry?

Chapter Preface   94

1. Whitewashing in Cinema Takes Many Forms   97
   Lester Andrist
2. *Black Panther* Was a Watershed Moment in Cinema— *Wakanda Forever* May Be Another   103
   César Albarrán Torres and Liam Burke
3. Hollywood Has a Long History of Whitewashing   108
   Dolores Tierney
4. Why Blackface Endures   113
   Gene Demby and Rachel Martin
5. In Defense of Cross-Cultural Casting   119
   Bob Mondello

Periodical and Internet Sources Bibliography   126

Chapter 4: Are Team Names and Mascots that Use Cultural Appropriation Acceptable?

Chapter Preface   129

1. Native American Mascots and Team Names Are Common in the U.S. and Europe, but That Is Finally Changing   132
   Sam Hitchmough

2. Ten Controversial Sports Team Names that Have
   Been or Should Be Changed **138**
   Justin Findlay
3. Progress Is Being Made in Changing Offensive
   Team Names **143**
   Encyclopædia Britannica
4. Native American Mascots Reinforce Negative
   Stereotypes **148**
   Justin Angle
5. Team Names Should Foster Positive Energy,
   Not Negative Racist Energy **153**
   Paul Whitinui

Periodical and Internet Sources Bibliography **160**

For Further Discussion **162**
Organizations to Contact **164**
Bibliography of Books **169**
Index **171**

The Importance of Opposing Viewpoints

Perhaps every generation experiences a period in time in which the populace seems especially polarized, starkly divided on the important issues of the day and gravitating toward the far ends of the political spectrum and away from a consensus-facilitating middle ground. The world that today's students are growing up in and that they will soon enter into as active and engaged citizens is deeply fragmented in just this way. Issues relating to terrorism, immigration, women's rights, minority rights, race relations, health care, taxation, wealth and poverty, the environment, policing, military intervention, the proper role of government—in some ways, perennial issues that are freshly and uniquely urgent and vital with each new generation—are currently roiling the world.

If we are to foster a knowledgeable, responsible, active, and engaged citizenry among today's youth, we must provide them with the intellectual, interpretive, and critical-thinking tools and experience necessary to make sense of the world around them and of the all-important debates and arguments that inform it. After all, the outcome of these debates will in large measure determine the future course, prospects, and outcomes of the world and its peoples, particularly its youth. If they are to become successful members of society and productive and informed citizens, students need to learn how to evaluate the strengths and weaknesses of someone else's arguments, how to sift fact from opinion and fallacy, and how to test the relative merits and validity of their own opinions against the known facts and the best possible available information. The landmark series Opposing Viewpoints has been providing students with just such critical-thinking skills and exposure to the debates surrounding society's most urgent contemporary issues for many years, and it continues to serve this essential role with undiminished commitment, care, and rigor.

The key to the series's success in achieving its goal of sharpening students' critical-thinking and analytic skills resides in its title—

Opposing Viewpoints. In every intriguing, compelling, and engaging volume of this series, readers are presented with the widest possible spectrum of distinct viewpoints, expert opinions, and informed argumentation and commentary, supplied by some of today's leading academics, thinkers, analysts, politicians, policy makers, economists, activists, change agents, and advocates. Every opinion and argument anthologized here is presented objectively and accorded respect. There is no editorializing in any introductory text or in the arrangement and order of the pieces. No piece is included as a "straw man," an easy ideological target for cheap point-scoring. As wide and inclusive a range of viewpoints as possible is offered, with no privileging of one particular political ideology or cultural perspective over another. It is left to each individual reader to evaluate the relative merits of each argument—as they see it, and with the use of ever-growing critical-thinking skills—and grapple with their own assumptions, beliefs, and perspectives to determine how convincing or successful any given argument is and how the reader's own stance on the issue may be modified or altered in response to it.

This process is facilitated and supported by volume, chapter, and selection introductions that provide readers with the essential context they need to begin engaging with the spotlighted issues, with the debates surrounding them, and with their own perhaps shifting or nascent opinions on them. In addition, guided reading and discussion questions encourage readers to determine the authors' point of view and purpose, interrogate and analyze the various arguments and their rhetoric and structure, evaluate the arguments' strengths and weaknesses, test their claims against available facts and evidence, judge the validity of the reasoning, and bring into clearer, sharper focus the reader's own beliefs and conclusions and how they may differ from or align with those in the collection or those of their classmates.

Research has shown that reading comprehension skills improve dramatically when students are provided with compelling, intriguing, and relevant "discussable" texts. The subject matter of these collections could not be more compelling, intriguing, or urgently relevant to today's students and the world they are poised to inherit. The anthologized articles and the reading and discussion questions that are included with them also provide the basis for stimulating, lively, and passionate classroom debates. Students who are compelled to anticipate objections to their own argument and identify the flaws in those of an opponent read more carefully, think more critically, and steep themselves in relevant context, facts, and information more thoroughly. In short, using discussable text of the kind provided by every single volume in the Opposing Viewpoints series encourages close reading, facilitates reading comprehension, fosters research, strengthens critical thinking, and greatly enlivens and energizes classroom discussion and participation. The entire learning process is deepened, extended, and strengthened.

For all of these reasons, Opposing Viewpoints continues to be exactly the right resource at exactly the right time—when we most need to provide readers with the critical-thinking tools and skills that will not only serve them well in school but also in their careers and their daily lives as decision-making family members, community members, and citizens. This series encourages respectful engagement with and analysis of opposing viewpoints and fosters a resulting increase in the strength and rigor of one's own opinions and stances. As such, it helps make readers "future ready," and that readiness will pay rich dividends for the readers themselves, for the citizenry, for our society, and for the world at large.

Introduction

> "All cultures learn from each other. The problem is that if the Beatles tell me that they learned everything they know from Blind Willie, I want to know why Blind Willie is still running an elevator in Jackson, Mississippi."
>
> —Amiri Baraka

In a speech delivered at the Brisbane Writing Festival in 2016, Lionel Shriver, author of the popular novel *We Need to Talk About Kevin* and numerous other books, made this declaration:

> I am hopeful that the concept of "cultural appropriation" is a passing fad: people with different backgrounds rubbing up against each other and exchanging ideas and practices is self-evidently one of the most productive, fascinating aspects of modern urban life.

As a novelist, Shriver took umbrage with the way in which accusations of cultural appropriation have become a form of censorship. At its extreme, such criticism threatens the very act of creating fiction itself, she believes. If writers can only create stories about their own experiences, from the point of view of people similar to themselves, fiction loses its ability to explore, among other things. Taken to its logical extreme, Shriver writes,

> Someone like me only permits herself to write from the perspective of a straight white female born in North Carolina, closing on sixty, able-bodied but with bad knees, skint for years but finally able to buy the odd new shirt. All that's left is memoir.

Shriver cites a number of books that could not have been written according to today's rules: one in particular, *Black Like Me*, is about a white man who darkens his skin to understand what it was like to be Black in the Jim Crow South. This famous book had a tremendous impact on our understanding of racism when it was published. Today? It likely couldn't have been written—or at least, published by a reputable press.

Many who listened to Shriver's speech that day in Brisbane, Australia, were offended. Ironically, this type of quick-to-take-offense "gotcha" criticism was exactly what Shriver was writing about. After her speech, according to a *New York Times* article, a festival participant accosted Shriver, shouting, "How dare you come to my country and offend our minorities?" Shriver said that the woman had clearly not actually heard her speech, which made no mention of Australian minorities.

But other criticisms come from a more considered angle. Sudanese-born Australian social activist Yassmin Abdel-Magied, an attendee at the festival where Shriver spoke, walked out on the speech. She later wrote that Shriver's talk was "a celebration of the unfettered exploitation of the experiences of others, under the guise of fiction."

To be fair, in her speech, Shriver offers many over-the-top, and sometimes ludicrous, examples of cultural appropriation policing. She mentions a Canadian yoga teacher who was shamed into suspending her class because yoga appropriates Indian culture. Shriver further cites a student protest at Oberlin College in Ohio against serving "culturally appropriated food" like sushi in their dining hall because doing so is insensitive to Japanese people.

Like any new concept, cultural appropriation has to work itself through our society, and sometimes there are extreme reactions to it, both pro and con. The animus against sushi and yoga would seem to be part of that extreme reaction. After all, as Shriver notes, is every Mexican food restaurant in the United States supposed to shut down or at least eliminate potentially offensive iconography such as sombreros?

Key questions about cultural appropriation have yet to be answered: what are the rules, and who is responsible for making them? We could say that authors, musicians, filmmakers, and other creators should use common sense when it comes to taking material from other cultures. We could say that they should show respect and honor those cultures. But every work of fiction, if it's any good, has likely offended someone, somewhere. And any team mascot, or musical composition, or film might do the same. Who is in charge of determining whether material is offensive? People on social media? A college board of directors?

Cultural appropriation is a fascinating subject for the very reason that it is subjective. One person's ceiling is another's floor. For every offended person, there are ten more who don't worry about the issue. For years, the Washington "Redskins" ownership insisted that Native Americans themselves were not offended by the racist name. But they were clearly cherry-picking their responses. Many were offended, to the point where the name was eventually replaced.

Shriver makes some reasonable points about how language is policed and how identity politics can be taken to extreme lengths. But she fails to take note of all the ways in which the conversation around cultural appropriation has been a positive force for change. Because, at its core, cultural appropriation is not about who can wear what hat, or eat what delicacy, or even write which character—cultural appropriation is about power and money. We could add "respect" to that duo, but it usually comes with power and money.

Cultural appropriation is why Big Mama Thornton did not initially get publishing royalties for her song "Ball and Chain," but had to wait until a white artist, Janis Joplin, recorded it. Cultural appropriation is about thousands of Atlanta Braves fans performing the "tomahawk chop" at baseball games, an act that perpetuates stereotypical and violent images of Native Americans. And cultural appropriation is about how actor Mickey Rooney caricatured an Asian man in the film *Breakfast at Tiffany's* by taping up his eyes, wearing buck teeth, and affecting a ridiculous accent.

Examples like those above are serious breaches of ethical and tasteful conduct, even though, in their day, they were not necessarily seen as such. The notion of cultural appropriation, at its best, can right serious wrongs. At its worst, as Shriver suggests, it can lead to unnecessary censorship.

Opposing Viewpoints: Cultural Appropriation presents a wide range of opinions that debate and clarify the ethics and guidelines with respect to cultural borrowing. Conservative as well as progressive views on cultural appropriation are presented, as well as those in between. Many viewpoints included within offer possible solutions to the ethical quandaries involved in this complex issue.

CHAPTER 1

Is Cultural Appropriation Insult or Homage?

Chapter Preface

In one episode of the situational comedy *Seinfeld*, Jerry Seinfeld runs into his dentist, Tim Whatley, at a diner. Whatley, played by future *Breaking Bad* star Bryan Cranston, announces to the Jewish Jerry Seinfeld, "I'm a Jew." Apparently, Whatley has converted from Catholicism to Judaism.

When Jerry goes to Whatley for a cavity, the dentist proceeds to make a joke about (now deceased) actress Raquel Welch and a rabbi. Jerry is surprised. Whatley has been a Jew for only two days and already he's making fun of the culture. When Seinfeld shows surprise at this, saying, "Tim, do you think you should be making jokes like that?" the dentist replies, "Why not, I'm Jewish, remember?" He then adds, "Jerry, it's our sense of humor that has sustained us as a people for 3,000 years." "5,000," says Jerry, correcting him.

Later, Jerry seeks out a priest who is also a patient of Whatley's and complains to the holy man that Whatley is making Jewish jokes.

"And this offends you as a Jew," says the priest.

"No, it offends me as a comedian," Jerry says, a clever line that inverts the obvious offense.

Although the concept wasn't broadly recognized in the 1990s, Tim Whatley is clearly performing a textbook example of cultural appropriation. This, of course, is not what offends Jerry, since in 1990 he more than likely had never heard of the phrase. Instead Jerry suspects that as a former Catholic turned Jew, Whatley can safely make jokes that most people cannot, and thus gets "total joke immunity." What really makes Whatley guilty of cultural appropriation, though, is that he's apparently become a Jew without the slightest knowledge of Jewish history, as his shortening of Jewish history by two millennia suggests. One might say that Whatley's conversion shows his high regard for Jewish culture, but Jerry suspects that he's converted to Judaism "for the jokes."

Whatley's cultural appropriation of jokes from a minority group that really has suffered throughout history is here played for laughs. But Whatley represents a very common type of people with regard to cultural appropriation: those who believe, or at least pretend, that they are honoring or appreciating a culture, when in actuality they are only using it for their own ends.

In reality the process of converting to Judaism is not easy. Depending on the rules of each Jewish denomination, it may involve extensive study and participation in Jewish services. If Whatley had truly followed the laws for conversion to Judaism, he might well have been an appreciator of the culture. But the comedic situation required that his conversion was superficial—as indicated in his mistake about Jewish history (which, as of 2024, is in the Hebrew year 5784).

As explained on the University of Wisconsin's website, cultural appreciation

> can be described as a way of honoring another culture through exploration and seeking an understanding as a way to honor that culture, beliefs, and traditions. There is a thin line between Cultural Appreciation and Cultural Appropriation. If one uses the knowledge that they have learned for personal gain, they have crossed that thin line.

Whatley clearly crosses that thin line when he uses his conversion to Judaism "for the jokes."

But those who cross the line often rationalize their behavior as cultural appreciation. Famous British guitarist Eric Clapton, for example, who always believed that he, in his own words, "championed Black music," went on a racist, anti-immigrant tirade onstage in 1976. At the time he was reaping the financial rewards of his 1974 cover of Jamaican artist Bob Marley's reggae anthem "I Shot the Sheriff" having gone to number one on the Billboard charts. Clapton's career was built on covering Black musicians such as Robert Johnson (of "Crossroads Blues" fame) and Muddy Waters.

More recently, white Australian rapper Iggy Azalea has answered charges of cultural appropriation by saying that, "I wanted to talk so much about my experiences of things I didn't have, and I think it felt like I wasn't acknowledging that there is white privilege and there is institutionalized racism." She added, "It seemed to a lot of people like I was living in this bubble or unaware of all these things that people have to experience."

Nevertheless, Azalea belies this statement of cultural appreciation by pushing her appropriation of Black culture even further in order to reap massive financial rewards. After the release of her 2021 record "I Am the Stripclub," many accused her of blackfishing or "imitating a Black female aesthetic" by darkening her skin and donning a black wig. Azalea—and her makeup artist—deny the accusations. In the video, she looks strikingly like reality television star Kim Kardashian, another rich white woman who has profited off cultural appropriation.

Clearly, when there is money involved—and not merely ethnic jokes—the line between cultural appreciation and cultural appropriation can blur into meaninglessness.

VIEWPOINT 1

> "There's a difference between appreciating a culture, which might include enjoying food from another country or learning a new language, and appropriating it which involves taking something 'without authority or right'."

How Cultural Appropriation Is Defined

Encyclopædia Britannica

The following viewpoint provides a working definition of cultural appropriation, separating it from harmless cultural appreciation, and adds a number of insightful examples of harmful cultural appropriation. Examples usually focus on a majority group member who exploits minority culture for personal gain or other satisfaction. Marginalized groups are usually the victims of such appropriation, whether they belong to Black, LGBTQIA+, Native American, or other groups. The Encyclopædia Britannica, *which is Latin for "British Encyclopedia," is a general knowledge English-language encyclopedia. It has been published since 1768.*

As you read, consider the following questions:

1. Where did the term "cultural appropriation" originate and how did it gain widespread acceptance?

"What Is Cultural Appropriation?," Britannica. Reprinted by permission.

2. What working definition of cultural appropriation does the viewpoint provide?
3. What factors were involved in Madonna's cultural appropriation of a dance?

You hear about it on Twitter, in news headlines, and at Thanksgiving dinner. But what is cultural appropriation, anyway?

It's not a concept designed to trick you. Taking off in the 1980s, the term *cultural appropriation* was first used in academic spaces to discuss issues such as colonialism and the relationships between majority and minority groups. Like many such terms, *cultural appropriation* eventually made its way out of the academy and into popular culture. (Other examples include *gaslighting*, an elaborate, all-encompassing form of deception, and *triggering*, "to cause," as *Merriam-Webster* defines it, "an intense and usually negative emotional reaction in someone." Both spent time as mainly academic words before gaining broader usage both online and off.)

Cultural appropriation takes place when members of a majority group adopt cultural elements of a minority group in an exploitative, disrespectful, or stereotypical way. To fully understand its consequences, though, we need to make sure we have a working definition of *culture* itself.

What Makes Cultural Appropriation Inappropriate?

How Cultural Appropriation Contributes to the Endangerment of Indigenous Women

When someone from one culture chooses to emulate members of another culture for entertainment, it is more than culturally disrespectful.

continued on next spread

The example of the "sexy Native" costume that appears every Halloween also perpetuates harmful and dangerous stereotypes that contribute to sexual violence against and human trafficking of Indigenous women and girls.

When a woman of non-Indigenous heritage dresses up as the "sexy native", she demeans Indigenous women and insults the hundreds of missing and murdered Indigenous women and all those who loved them. She is, unwittingly, contributing to the endangerment of Indigenous women and girls.

We are hopeful that in this era of reconciliation, there will be fewer retail outlets and customers who choose culturally inappropriate merchandise. We know it's possible as there has been so much progress in reconciliation on so many fronts but we realize there is still work ahead.

Imitation Is Flattery

Some say imitation is the finest form of flattery, which may be true in some cases. However, there are still challenges created by those who choose to emulate aspects of Indigenous culture for entertainment without knowledge of the specific Indigenous culture related to the item, or an understanding of the history and worldview of that culture.

Perpetuating Stereotypes

We've talked about the "sexy Native." Now let's look at those who buy an ersatz feathered headdress to go with their polyester "buckskin" chief costume. I'm sure that those who bought these items have never studied the regalia of hereditary chiefs. They are likely unaware of the symbolism of the feathers. And they are probably unaware that the feathered headdress is not a pan-Indigenous form of headdress or that the regalia of chiefs on the West Coast is as different from chiefs in the East as it is different from chiefs on the plains.

As Canada moves along the reconciliation continuum, we hope that all will want to learn about Indigenous Peoples, their cultures, their pre-contact lives, and the impact of colonization. It is through education that people will understand that Indigenous Peoples have struggled to protect and preserve their culture, and how they were forced to change the way they lived, spoke, celebrated, and worshiped.

> When understanding what cultural appropriation is, why it's harmful, disrespectful, and can even contribute to endangering Indigenous women and girls becomes universal, then as a country, we can celebrate.
>
> "Why Cultural Appropriation Is Disrespectful," Indigenous Corporate Training, October 4, 2020.

Historically, deciding exactly what culture is hasn't been easy. The earliest and most quoted anthropological explanation comes from English anthropologist Edward Burnett Tylor, who wrote in 1871 that "culture…is that complex whole which includes knowledge, belief, art, morals, law, custom, and any other capabilities and habits acquired by man as a member of society." Tylor explains that culture isn't biologically inherited. Rather, it's the things you learn and do when you belong to a particular group.

It may not be immediately obvious from Tylor's definition why adopting elements from another culture can be harmful. But there's a difference between *appreciating* a culture, which might include enjoying food from another country or learning a new language, and *appropriating* it which involves taking something "without authority or right," as *Merriam-Webster* explains.

Let's explore a few different ways cultural appropriation can be perpetuated, taken from a largely American context:

A member of a majority group profiting financially or socially from the culture of a minority group is cultural appropriation. In 1990 Madonna released the music video for her song "Vogue," which featured a dance (*voguing*) developed in the gay drag-ball subculture. Though Madonna included drag performers in the video, ostensibly respecting the dance's origins, she was the one who profited when "Vogue" went double platinum in the United States. Because Madonna gained financial and cultural capital from *voguing* in a way that its creators did not, her use of the dance was cultural appropriation.

A member of a majority group oversimplifying the culture of a minority group, or treating the culture of a minority group as a joke, is cultural appropriation. When the first iteration of the Cleveland Indians baseball team formed in 1915, the *Cleveland Plain Dealer* newspaper wrote: "There will be no real Indians on the roster, but the name will recall fine traditions." Though not intended as criticism at the time, that sentence neatly explains the problem with a concept like Native American sports mascots: they are not a product of actual indigenous cultures, but they represent what non-indigenous people assume indigenous cultures to be. Because these mascots rely on racial caricature and perpetuate false stereotypes of Native Americans, they function as cultural appropriation.

A member of a majority group separating a cultural element of a minority group from its original meaning is cultural appropriation. In the 2010s the rise of music festivals such as Coachella sparked new trends in festival fashion, including Native American warbonnets worn as headdresses. Unlike traditional Native American jewelry, much of which is sold by indigenous artists to customers of all cultures, these feathered headdresses hold a significant cultural purpose. Among Plains Indian communities, warbonnets are worn only by community leaders on special occasions; in other groups, they're an earned honour not unlike a military medal. Because they separate the warbonnet from its original cultural meaning, non-indigenous festival attendees wearing Native American headdresses are practicing cultural appropriation.

A member of a majority group adopting an element of a minority culture without consequences while members of the minority group face backlash for the same cultural element is cultural appropriation. Dreadlocks have long been associated with Black culture—though it's easy to find non-Black people wearing the style as well. Historically, though, Black people have faced discrimination for wearing traditionally Black hairstyles including locs: Black people with locs have been barred from walking at high-school graduations, denied jobs, wrongfully associated with drug use, and otherwise discriminated against. As a result of systemic racism, Black people face consequences for wearing dreadlocks that non-Black people do not. Non-Black people wearing their hair in dreadlocks is cultural appropriation.

As these examples show, the consequences of cultural appropriation can be wide-ranging. But they're all ultimately the result of a more powerful person's lack of thoughtful, respectful engagement with others—a dynamic that's harmful whether it is intentional or not.

VIEWPOINT 2

> *"But how does creating gated cultures, and preventing others from trespassing upon one's culture without permission, challenge racism or promote social justice?"*

Self-Appointed Gatekeepers of Culture Are Dangerous

Kenan Malik

In this viewpoint, Kenan Malik comments on the current proliferation of cultural appropriation accusations. He traces the history of concepts of "culture" and how these concepts have evolved from celebrating the spirit of a country or people into gatekeeping and shaming those who desire to participate. This latter behavior, Malik argues, actually perpetuates stereotypes, doing more harm than good. The campaign against cultural appropriation is, he believes, "part of the broader attempt to police communities and cultures." For Malik, the fight against injustice must center on removing self-appointed gatekeepers of culture. Kenan Malik is a London-based writer, broadcaster, and lecturer. He is the author of numerous books, including The Quest for a Moral Compass: A Global History of Ethics *(2015).*

"The Bane of Cultural Appropriation," by Kenan Malik, Al Jazeera Media Network, April 14, 2016. Reprinted by permission.

As you read, consider the following questions:

1. What definition of "cultural appropriation" does Malik cite?
2. How is the question of who is policing cultural appropriation central to his argument?
3. Malik believes many of the cultural appropriation battles are silly and trivial. What policing and gatekeeping does he consider far more serious?

Another week, another controversy about "cultural appropriation." The latest has been the furor over Justin Bieber's dreadlocks. The Bieber furor followed similar controversies over Beyonce's Bollywood outfit, Kylie Jenner's cornrows, Canadians practising yoga, English students wearing sombreros and American students donning Native American Halloween costumes.

Many of these controversies may seem as laughable as Bieber's locks. What they reveal, however, is how degraded have become contemporary campaigns for social justice.

Cultural appropriation is, in the words of Susan Scafidi, professor of law at Fordham University, and author of Who Owns Culture? Appropriation and Authenticity in American Law, "Taking intellectual property, traditional knowledge, cultural expressions, or artifacts from someone else's culture without permission." This can include the "unauthorised use of another culture's dance, dress, music, language, folklore, cuisine, traditional medicine, religious symbols, etc."

A Colonial Past?

But what is it for knowledge or an object to "belong" to a culture? And who gives permission for someone from another culture to use such knowledge or forms?

The idea that the world could be divided into distinct cultures, and that every culture belonged to a particular people, has its roots in late 18th-century Europe.

The Romantic movement, which developed in part in opposition to the rationalism of the Enlightenment, celebrated cultural differences and insisted on the importance of "authentic" ways of being.

For Johann Gottfried Herder, the German philosopher who best articulated the Romantic notion of culture, what made each people – or "volk" – unique was its particular language, history and modes of living. The unique nature of each volk was expressed through its "volksgeist" – the unchanging spirit of a people refined through history.

Herder was no reactionary – he was an important champion of equality – but his ideas about culture were adopted by reactionary thinkers. Those ideas became central to racial thinking – the notion of the volksgeist was transformed into the concept of racial make-up – and fuelled the belief that non-Western societies were "backward" because of their "backward" cultures.

Radicals challenging racism and colonialism rejected the Romantic view of culture, adopting instead a universalist perspective. From the struggle against slavery to the anti-colonial movements, the aim not to protect one's own special culture but to create a more universal culture in which all could participate on equal terms.

Enters Identity Politics

In recent decades, however, the universalist viewpoint has eroded, largely as many of the social movements that embodied that viewpoint have disintegrated. The social space vacated by that disintegration became filled by identity politics.

As the broader struggles for social transformation have faded, people have tended to retreat into their particular faiths or cultures, and to embrace more parochial forms of identity. In this process, the old cultural arguments of the racists have returned, but now rebranded as "antiracist."

But how does creating gated cultures, and preventing others from trespassing upon one's culture without permission, challenge racism or promote social justice?

Campaigners against cultural appropriation argue that when "privileged" cultures adopt the styles of "less privileged" ones they help create stereotypes of what such cultures are like, and assert racial power.

"By dressing up as a fake Indian," one Native American told white students, "you are asserting your power over us, and continuing to oppress us."

The trouble is that in making the case against cultural appropriation, campaigners equally perpetuate stereotypes.

After all, to suggest that it is "authentic" for blacks to wear locks, or for Native Americans to wear a headdress, but not for whites to do so, is itself to stereotype those cultures.

Cultures do not, and cannot, work through notions of "ownership." The history of culture is the history of cultural appropriation – of cultures borrowing, stealing, changing, transforming.

Nor does preventing whites from wearing locks or practising yoga challenge racism in any meaningful way.

What the campaigns against cultural appropriation reveal is the disintegration of the meaning of "anti-racism." Once it meant to struggle for equal treatment for all.

Costumes and Cultural Appropriation

Halloween is a time for people to get creative and dress up as someone or something else. But Joshua Hunt, who is Cheyenne and a board member of the Lake Erie Native American Council, said it's not a time to make an entire culture your costume, otherwise known as cultural appropriation.

continued on next spread

Cultural Appropriation

"My identity is not a joke," said Hunt. "Ethnic and racial identities are not a costume. We cannot just take them off. So you might want to dress up as a Native American. But at the end of the day, you can take that off, whereas I can't take off my skin."

The dictionary definition of cultural appropriation is "the adoption, usually without acknowledgment, of cultural identity markers from subcultures or minority communities into mainstream culture by people with a relatively privileged status." Hunt said the feathers people wear on Halloween as a costume are sacred to Native American culture.

"Feathers or feather headdresses, those are given to people that have made large sacrifices for their communities. Native Americans see it the same way as Christians see the cross," said Hunt. "That's something that's given. That's earned like a medal of honor. So when it's taken and turned into a play thing, or a costume, it's disrespected. No one would wear a medal of honor that didn't earn it."

The feather headdress is just one example. Wearing things like a sombrero and a mustache, a hijab or an afro can all stereotype ethnic groups.

"Why are you dehumanizing a whole race of people? Why are you dehumanizing people? You shouldn't be doing that. You shouldn't be teaching your children that it's OK to stereotype, disrespect and dehumanize whole groups of marginalized people," said Hunt. "That's especially bad since there's an epidemic of missing and murdered Indigenous women. When you take Native American women and objectify them, dehumanize them (or) sexualize them, you're contributing to that epidemic."

There are gray areas, but there's also a line, Hunt said.

Hunt said some costumes should be avoided altogether because of the deeper meaning behind certain outfits. He said knowing the whole historical context is very important.

[...]

"Just because you legally can doesn't mean that you should," said Hunt. "I shouldn't do those things on moral and ethical grounds because it's wrong. It is harmful. This has to stop now. It starts and stops with you — the adults, the parents, teachers, etc."

"Can I wear that? What to know about culturally insensitive Halloween costumes," by Taylor Bruck, Spectrum News 1, October 28, 2021.

Now it means defining the correct etiquette for a plural society. The campaign against cultural appropriation is about policing manners rather than transforming society.

Who Is the Authority?

This takes us to the second question: who does the policing? Who gives permission for people of other cultures to use particular cultural forms? Who acts as the gatekeepers to gated cultures?

Most black people could probably not care less what Justin Bieber does to his hair. Inevitably, the gatekeepers are those who are outraged by Bieber's locks.

The very fact of being outraged makes one the arbiter of what is outrageous. The gatekeepers, in other words, define themselves, because they are ones who want to put up the gates.

The debates around Justin Bieber's hair or Beyonce's Bollywood outfit are relatively trivial. But, in other contexts, the creation of gatekeepers has proved highly problematic.

In many European nations, minority groups have come to be seen as distinct communities, each with their own interests, needs and desires, and each with certain so-called "community leaders" acting as their representatives.

Such leaders are frequently religious, often conservative, and rarely representative of their communities. But they wield great power as mediators between their communities and wider society. In effect, they act as gatekeepers to those communities.

Their role as gatekeepers is particularly problematic when it comes to policing not fashion styles or cuisine but ideas. Community leaders often help define what is acceptable to say about particular communities, and what is "offensive."

And notions of "offence" are often used to police not just what outsiders may say about a particular community, but to shut down debate within those communities – think of the fatwa against Salman Rushdie or the shutting down by Sikh activists of Sikh playwright Gurpreet Kaur Bhatti's play *Behzti*, which explored the role of women within Sikh communities.

The campaign against cultural appropriation is, in other words, part of the broader attempt to police communities and cultures. Those who most suffer from such policing are minority communities themselves, and in particular progressive voices within those communities.

The real fight against injustice begins with ridding ourselves of our self-appointed gatekeepers.

Viewpoint 3

> *"Scholarly consensus regarding cultural appropriation has long accepted that the lines between cultural appreciation and appropriation may be difficult to clearly determine in real time, and especially within the contemporary social media-driven zeitgeist."*

There Is a Fine Line Between Cultural Appropriation and Cultural Appreciation

Joshua E. Kane

In this viewpoint, Joshua Kane writes about how it is sometimes difficult to separate cultural appreciation and cultural appropriation. He cites a number of blatant examples of appropriation by celebrities such as Justin Bieber and the Kardashians. But Kane's focus in the viewpoint is on a liquor promoted by Black actor Michael B. Jordan of Black Panther fame. The beverage in question, formerly named "J'ouvert," uses Trinidadian culture in its marketing. The controversy was notable for not being one-sided. Many stepped up to defend Jordan as well as to condemn him. The name of the beverage was ultimately changed, but Kane believes that if Jordan had truly immersed himself in the culture of Trinidad, he might have avoided the criticism. Joshua Kane is currently a lecturer in sociology and

"What is cultural appropriation, and how does it differ from cultural appreciation?," by Joshua E. Kane, The Conversation, July 7, 2021. https://theconversation.com/what-is-cultural-appropriation-and-how-does-it-differ-from-cultural-appreciation-162331. Licensed under CC BY-ND 4.0 International.

integrative social science at Arizona State University in the College of Integrative Science and Arts and Chair of the CISA Antiracism Textbook Taskforce.

As you read, consider the following questions:

1. How are fashion companies transgressing when it comes to cultural appropriation?
2. How did Edward Said and George Lipsitz help give birth to our contemporary notion of cultural appropriation?
3. When, according to the viewpoint, is cultural sharing best?

Fashion companies are increasingly being taken to task for selling expensive versions of traditional Indigenous dress. Gucci's kaftans came with a US$3,500 price tag, which is far more than the $10 that Indians pay for a very similar-looking traditional kurta. Louis Vuitton's $700 scarfs resembled the keiffyeh that is viewed as a symbol of Palestinian nationalism and sold in much of the Arab world at a far lower cost. Both fashion labels received criticism, but not only for the seemingly inflated prices. They were accused of appropriating Indigenous cultural artifacts for profit.

It is also an accusation that has been leveled against many celebrities. The American model Kendall Jenner was accused of "hijacking Mexican culture and wearing it as a costume" for her new Tequila 818 advertising campaign. And Canadian singer Justin Bieber is yet again being accused of cultural appropriation for sporting dreadlocks – a natural hairstyle for people of color across many different civilizations.

These are just a few examples of the increasing global phenomenon of people, organizations and businesses being held to account for appropriating cultures outside of their own. Interestingly, though, the boundaries between ethical cultural sharing and exploitative cultural appropriation are not always clear.

I am a scholar researching American race and ethnic relations, and students often ask me how they can differentiate between the two.

What Is Cultural Appropriation?

In the halls of academia, discourse regarding cultural appropriation arose in the late 1970s, sparked by the publication of Edward Said's famous book "Orientalism." In this work, Said explored how, in the West, cultural notions of the "orient" invariably aided and abetted the material and cultural plundering of Asia.

As research on the history of Western cultural exploitation of Indigenous peoples proliferated, the work and research of American historian and cultural theorist George Lipsitz came to be viewed as laying the foundation for today's debates regarding what is and what is not cultural appropriation.

Lipsitz, writing in the 1990s, argued that cultural appreciation becomes cultural appropriation "when an element of culture is adopted from a marginalized group without respect for its cultural meaning or significance or with the purpose of exploiting the culture for economic or social gain."

That being said, scholarly consensus regarding cultural appropriation has long accepted that the lines between cultural appreciation and appropriation may be difficult to clearly determine in real time, and especially within the contemporary social media-driven zeitgeist.

Thin Line

There have been myriad cases of cultural appropriation of Indigenous and traditional cultures. However, some cases appear to be more clearly unethical and exploitative of culture than others.

The vast plundering of Indigenous cultural artifacts, treasures and traditions that occurred throughout the colonial era provides the clearest historical examples of unconscionable exploitation and appropriation of Indigenous cultures. And, for the most part, the treasures still have not been returned.

A more recent example of clearly unethical cultural appropriation and exploitation of Indigenous cultures for profit came to the fore in 2021 when the government of Mexico accused clothing companies Zara, Anthropologie and Patowl of appropriating and selling designs based on patterns and symbols derived from indigenous Mexican cultures and demanded recompense.

The line blurs a bit when celebrity influencers unwittingly appropriate and inappropriately flaunt sacred symbols of Indigenous and traditional cultures – as in the case of Kim Kardashian sporting earrings patterned from the sacred Hindu Om symbol during a photo shoot for her beauty products line. In another example, lingerie company Victoria's Secret has repeatedly used designs inspired by sacred Native American traditions during its fashion shows.

A similar case of blurred lines between cultural appreciation and appropriation arose just last month when actor Michael B. Jordan announced on the U.S. holiday Juneteenth the launch of his new rum brand J'ouvert. The name derives from the Trinidadian word for the early morning celebrations kicking off the nation's annual Emancipation Day – a holiday marking the abolition of slavery in the Caribbean in 1838.

The marketing campaign for Jordan's rum reduced this important Trindadian holiday to the tagline – "J'OUVERT Rum is a tribute to the party start," provoking wide condemnation from Trinidadians, including Trinidadian rapper Nicki Minaj.

In support of Jordan and the rum's name, some Trinidadians pointed out that one of Jordan's business partners is Trinidadian and that Trinidad as a nation benefits from the exposure. Some social media commentators argued that the criticism may be misguided because, although Jordan may not be from Trinidad, he is Black, and diverse Black cultures should unite broadly in support of Black capitalism more generally.

Nevertheless, after a few days of contemplation, Jordan and his business partners apologized and opted to rebrand their rum.

Cultures Are Complex

The reality is that adjudicating between cultural appreciation and appropriation is never simple, and that is because cultures are vast, complex, historically determined and ever-changing.

In the cases of both Kardashian and Jordan, I would argue that had either of them sought to establish true cultural appreciation for the cultures from which they were drawing, the accusations and inappropriate use of cultural symbols could have been avoided. This could have been achieved through long immersion and deep learning over the years about the history and current manifestations of the cultures.

Americans are increasingly living within fantastically diverse multicultural worlds. Sharing in each others' cultures is not only good; when done right, it is important and helps build community.

But cultural sharing is best when done mindfully. And cultural appreciation is best when it is not ephemeral or fad-inspired.

VIEWPOINT 4

> *"If culture is anything, it is about constructing the meaning of things and events for a group—and this is necessarily rooted in place and time. Remove the culture from the context and it is diminished, or negated."*

Context Is Everything When It Comes to Borrowing Culture

Andy Pratt

Andy Pratt writes that context is key to understanding the difference between cultural appreciation and cultural appropriation. He cites the example of his wearing a religious symbol from another culture— the hijab—as a case of inappropriate borrowing. But to rule out all cases of cultural borrowing is to limit creativity and newness. Pratt believes that sensitivity toward other cultures is important. Asking for advice from those whose culture is impacted is a good step toward this sensitivity and inclusion. Andy Pratt is a professor of cultural economy at the University of London. He has worked as a consultant and advisor for national and urban policymakers, the EU, UNESCO, UNCTAD, WIPO, and the British Council.

"Cultural appropriation: theft or fair exchange?," by Andy Pratt, The Conversation, April 10, 2017. https://theconversation.com/cultural-appropriation-theft-or-fair-exchange-74892. Licensed under CC BY-ND 4.0 International.

Is Cultural Appropriation Insult or Homage?

As you read, consider the following questions:

1. Why, according to the viewpoint, was the painting *Open Casket* controversial?
2. What are three examples Pratt cites of people borrowing from other cultures?
3. Why does Pratt not consider the debate over cultural appropriation to be about censorship?

Imagine for a moment that I decided that as a fashion statement, and as a white atheist male, to choose to wear a hijab. Further imagine if, as a fashion blogger, I claimed that this was my new trend. We don't need much imagination to anticipate the outrage that it would cause – the problem is that the wrong person, is wearing it, in the wrong place and the wrong time.

Context is everything. The hijab is not simply a piece of black cloth, but one imbued with a set of meanings and symbols that have significance in this case both to a religion and its followers and, in a contrary manner, to another group of people who feel it symbolises a threat to their "way of life."

Culture, whether manifest as politics, everyday life, or religion is a sensitive topic. In this imaginary example I can be accused of not simply acting in an insensitive way – but seeking to appropriate, to steal or to claim as my own, the symbols and appearance of other groups. The offence caused is not simply misattribution, but undermining – or what might be perceived as mocking – the cultural and religious significance of the hijab.

Examples of this issue confront us every day; a real current example concerns the (white) artist Dana Schutz's painting *Open Casket* (2016) which depicts 14-year-old Emmett Till, who was lynched in Mississippi in 1955, lying in his coffin. Till's mother, Mamie Till Bradley, had insisted her son be buried in an open casket so that the world could see his horrifying injuries.

The press photographs taken at his funeral became iconic images that helped drive the civil rights movement. Schutz's painting has drawn accusations of cultural appropriation of a symbolic event and image.

The debate hinges on whether this use of the image should be disallowed on the grounds of the topic being too "sacred", or due to the artist being white – could she fully appreciate the importance of the symbol? Till's mother is not happy either. She says her desire to tell the world what happened to her son doesn't cover Schutz's paintings.

Cultural Conversations

Particular cases are always complex. We need to be clear in our thinking and what is at issue. Does this mean that people should never share or adapt another culture's signs or symbols? Culture would be rendered static and dead if this were the case – we can all recognise that new culture arises from the "conversation" with other cultures, or those traditions of the past. Think of fine art, music or writing.

Most US and UK rock and roll bears the DNA of the delta blues musicians who innovated the form. However, respect was not always paid to these originators by many musicians who often treated it as a common property. There is a line to be drawn between respect and disrespect.

Many of us have marveled at the Elgin marbles in the British Museum. But how did they come to be there. We can't properly call Lord Elgin's removal of the sculptures from the Parthenon theft as there is a dispute over claims that Elgin had legal title from the Ottoman empire. But is this not at the very least cultural appropriation?

If culture is anything, it is about constructing the meaning of things and events for a group – and this is necessarily rooted in place and time. Remove the "culture" from the context and it is diminished, or negated. Hence, the example of me wearing a Hijab, or perhaps Elgin displaying the Parthenon marbles in his front room. However, we commonly accept other positions.

So, if I take a melody, or an image, or phrase I can use it, sample it, or quote – if I get permission. The rights of the author extend to control how that cultural idea is expressed, but particularly the context – the concern is to maintain the integrity of the art. This second position is what we might call cultural exchange, based on an agreed usage in a particular context – one that the author agrees respects the original.

A third possibility is that there is a new cultural creation formed from a dialogue between the different cultural forms, one that engages with the meanings of the originals and forges new ones from them. Here the cultural product is neither one, nor the other or the originals – nor is it a licensed reuse or copy. This is the essence of creativity and how newness enters the world.

Culture of Creativity

Last month Nike produced a new product, its sport hijab. Is it offensive, is it cultural appropriation by a multinational? I'm not going to judge everybody's response to this, but I think this falls into the second category – and maybe the third, a new cultural creation. It was designed in collaboration with hijab wearers and religious authorities, as well as Nike.

Perhaps a more radical and innovative act was the development of the burkini, a classic attempt to take two different cultural traditions and innovate at the same time. Just as with regular swimwear, context is all – wearing it in the office is likely to cause offence.

The debate is not simply one of censorship. It is the subject position that matters (who is saying or doing the act), whose "traditions" or "culture" are being used – and with whose permission. Culture and meanings do not exist outside society and meanings depend on respecting the views of those concerned. In the Schutz case, this should mean consulting Mamie Till Bradley and the civil rights community. These are the voices needed to be part of a real debate, rather someone from outside the community whose idealised notion of what constitutes "censorship" has nothing to do with the rights or feelings of those concerned.

VIEWPOINT 5

> "When there is a lack of racial equality in a society, romanticising a marginalised group's objects, practices and modes of expression doesn't go both ways."

Cultural Appropriation Is Cultural Cannibalism

Jennifer Whitney

In this viewpoint, Jennifer Whitney discusses a 2017 controversy involving Selfridges, a popular British department store. The controversy involved an ad campaign in which two young white women sported braids and extensions, which was accused of appropriating Black culture and supporting a white standard of beauty. Whitney breaks down the arguments against this kind of appropriation, which include that there is an uneven playing field between cultures, that appropriation results in invisibility and exploitation for subjugated cultures, and that the meaning of aspects of one's culture get obscured or erased in the process of appropriation. Jennifer Whitney is a lecturer at Cardiff University in the UK.

"Braid rage: is cultural appropriation harmless borrowing or a damaging act?," by Jennifer Whitney, The Conversation, May 18, 2017, https://theconversation.com/braid-rage-is-cultural-appropriation-harmless-borrowing-or-a-damaging-act-77920. Licensed under CC BY-ND 4.0 International.

Is Cultural Appropriation Insult or Homage?

As you read, consider the following questions:

1. What examples does Whitney provide of cultural appropriation?
2. What does Whitney mean when she says there is an "un-level playing field" in cultural appropriation?
3. According to this viewpoint, what is the difference between cultural exchange and cultural appropriation?

Earlier this month, Selfridges, one of London's oldest and best-loved department stores, found itself embroiled in a political tangle over accusations of cultural appropriation.

Braid Bar, part of the store's Beauty Workshop, released its summer campaign, featuring Lila Grace Moss and Stella Jones – the daughters of supermodel Kate Moss and Clash guitarist Mick Jones respectively. With their hair styled in multiple braids with colourful extensions, the famous offspring were promoting the latest trends in festival fashion and beat-the-heat summer hair.

At first glance, such an enterprise might appear just to be fun, even frivolous. But fashion and beauty are never as superficial as they seem. Upon the release of the ad campaign, the Braid Bar found itself dealing with a knotty dilemma.

With white British models Moss and Jones as the faces of the ad campaign, Selfridges' Braid Bar has been accused of endorsing a white standard of beauty. Across social media, critics are calling out this lack of diversity while crucially noting Selfridges' additional miscalculation: the appropriation of black culture. The point being that this style of hair braiding is central to black female identity.

A Sorry Tale

Following the outcry, the Braid Bar released an apology:

> It has come to our attention that we have not given enough consideration to the cultures that we have drawn from in creating The Braid Bar, particularly black culture. Having been naive, our eyes are now open to the issues… We would like to reach

out and apologise to all of those who have been offended by our lack of cultural sensitivity... The Braid Bar is a welcoming and fun place for people of all races, ethnicities, genders, and ages; an environment that is all-inclusive and accessible to everyone. We are going to ensure that this ethos is reflected in everything we do and post from now on. We understand that it is our responsibility, as a company with a broad social media following, to teach and spread the knowledge of where these ideas, practices and skills originally come from and the stories that come with them.

The Braid Bar Instagram account was swiftly updated to include a photo of Janet Jackson in box braids (ironically, perhaps, from the 1993 film Poetic Justice), and several more photos of braid-sporting black women. Adding to the irony, the account also showcases a poster that states "never apologise for being who you are".

The Selfridges' Braid Bar controversy has not been confined to social media. Nor is it a one-off. Last year, the clothing brand Free People got into trouble for its Native American-inspired designs. Additionally, High School Musical actress Vanessa Hudgens recently came under scrutiny for wearing box braids as well.

Prompted by the buzz online, BBC Radio 4's Today programme hosted a short debate between Afua Hirsch and Tiffany Jenkins. Hirsch, a writer, broadcaster and barrister of Ghanaian Ashanti and English heritage, argued that cultural appropriation occurs when objects or practices of one culture are taken up by a different culture without acknowledgement of their source – or of their history. She suggested that this can lead to invisibility or financial exploitation.

In contrast, Jenkins, a British white writer and sociologist, argued that cultures borrow from one another out of respect and curiosity, and that to imply otherwise can lead to anxiety about everyday cultural exchange.

When taken up in mainstream media circles, the debate around cultural appropriation is often reduced to the following question: is cultural appropriation really just another name for cultural appreciation? Unfortunately, this is often where the discussion stops. Before we tease out the social and political implications of cultural appropriation, we need to take a look at the issues involved.

Cultural Cannibalism

Critics of cultural appropriation are not denying cultural exchange. Nor are we suggesting that differences should not be celebrated. Cultures are in constant dialogue, and there is always exchange that ensures an abundance of variety and fluidity in language, food, dance, music, fashion, and so on. This is inevitable. And, of course, diversity ought to be appreciated.

But what should we make of it when this type of exchange happens on an un-level playing field? With a history of racism, discrimination and empire that has a legacy in present day society, cultural appreciation starts to look more like what feminist scholar, bell hooks, author of *Ain't I a woman?: Black women and feminism* and *Black Looks* calls "cultural cannibalism".

That is, when there is a lack of racial equality in a society, romanticising a marginalised group's objects, practices and modes of expression doesn't go both ways. The cultural, historical, religious or political significance of objects, practices and modes of expression gets lost or obscured; meaning is not what tends to matter here. This not only leads to cultural invisibility, but can also promote further marginalisation and oppression.

Within a week of the Braid Bar summer ad campaign, two African American sisters in Malden, Massachusetts, faced detention and suspension from their high school for wearing box braids. One was banned from attending the school prom, while the other was removed from the school track and field team.

So, when a hairstyle like box braids or cornrows becomes trendy for mainstream white consumers only because a white model or celebrity wearing it makes it acceptably fashionable, then such a practice erases the cultural and historical origins of that style. It trivialises that culture and reduces it to a fashion fad.

As the ever-insightful *Teen Vogue* notes: "When Kylie sports cornrows at Coachella, it's considered 'edgy' and 'cool'. When black people wear cornrows, they get passed over for jobs and are asked to leave their classrooms."

That, in a nutshell, sums up the essential problem that cultural appropriation throws up, and why we need an honest, critical and high-profile discussion about it. Few would argue there is anything wrong with cultural exchange. What is wrong is when that exchange makes no reference, credit or acknowledgement to the culture it is borrowing from.

VIEWPOINT 6

> *"In the past, fashion design students would do extensive research to learn about materials and patterns as well as their origins before appropriating them. Now, anyone can access a database of images and take what they want without asking any questions."*

Cultural Appropriation Should Be Avoided
Copibec

This viewpoint covers how to avoid accusations of cultural appropriation. The piece begins by stating what cultural appropriation is not: eating food or listening to music from another culture is decidedly not cultural appropriation. Offense occurs when there isn't a level playing field, when someone from a privileged position in the power structure uses or profits from another, often minority, culture. According to the viewpoint, "For the dealings to be legitimate, the stakeholders have to be on a level playing field." The author then offers a number of ways in which cultural appropriation can be avoided. Copibec is a nonprofit social enterprise specializing in copyright management. Since its creation as a copyright collective in 1997, it has belonged to a community representing more than 30,000 authors and more than 1,300 publishers.

"How to avoid cultural appropriation," Copibec, October 11, 2022. Reprinted by permission.

As you read, consider the following questions:

1. How does power figure into the cultural appropriation dynamic?
2. How do certain Halloween costumes exemplify the phenomenon of cultural appropriation?
3. Why should creators "avoid the sacred"?

One of the basic rules when it comes to copyright is that you need to ask the copyright owner for permission before using the content they created.

Does that principle apply to cultural goods? Or can anything be used by anyone, however they want, without taking the community of origin into account?

First, What Is Cultural Appropriation?

Cultural appropriation is the reuse by an unauthorized individual of an element that belongs to a minority cultural group when that use is misinformed or is done against the will of the relevant group.

In our globalized world, people are becoming more and more aware of the complex relationships between different cultural communities, reflecting the inequalities among peoples and nations.

What's Not Meant by Cultural Appropriation?

Let's be clear! Eating food from another culture, listening to their music or trying to learn more about them is *not* cultural appropriation.

Instead, cultural appropriation occurs when the playing field isn't level: one of the stakeholders has an advantage or privilege or is simply more powerful than the other and can appropriate cultural goods without any consequence.

For the dealings to be legitimate, the stakeholders have to be on a level playing field.

Lack of Sensitivity

The reason cultural appropriation is criticized isn't because the intent is malicious, it's due to the damage caused to the community whose cultural practice is being borrowed.

Various communities are trying to reappropriate their history that's been impacted by colonialism and even slavery. They're still in the process of relearning to navigate their reality through ancient and sacred symbols.

The use of distinctive features from those communities, without taking their historical context into account, can show a lack of awareness.

Fashion Victim

Cultural appropriation for commercial purposes adds another layer to the impression of violation or desecration of the appropriated cultural identity.

In the past, fashion design students would do extensive research to learn about materials and patterns as well as their origins before appropriating them. Now, anyone can access a database of images and take what they want without asking any questions.

If a major Italian fashion house copies a traditional pattern from the Oma community of south Laos and makes it into a print replicated in multiple iterations, that action disregards all the work done by the community to create the pattern, the care they took in processing the materials, etc.

Dressing Up in Another Culture

Another example comes in the form of certain costumes worn at Halloween, which was initially an ancient Celtic celebration that used to mark the arrival of a new year.

> Halloween was originally a Celtic holiday that originated in Ireland to celebrate the new year. The Celtic calendar ended on October 31, the night of the lord of the dead, rather than December 31 as it does today. [Translation]
>
> — Léa Bitton, Savez-vous pourquoi nous célébrons Halloween ? (in French) from Paris Match

Making It a Commodity

Halloween exemplifies the phenomenon of cultural appropriation when some merrymakers show that they're "insensitive" by borrowing cultural emblems for their own amusement and wearing stereotypical costumes without any regard or appreciation for the communities where those cultural goods originate.

Using a feature from an exotic culture as a commodity can be perceived as disrespectful. Especially if that feature is considered sacred, such as ceremonial clothing.

5 Ways to Avoid Cultural Appropriation

Cultural appropriation is about attitude. It's in the approach: taking while offering nothing in return.

But what can be offered? We can give our open-mindedness, healthy curiosity, attention, goodwill in interacting with cultural communities, and efforts to do some research.

Here are 5 ways to avoid missteps:

1. Research the culture: Learn about the source of the cultural goods that interest you. What context do they occur in? What's their meaning historically?
2. Avoid the sacred: Certain objects or designs are reserved for sacred cultural practices and deserve more respect and reverence than others. A notable example is the First Nations headdress.
3. Don't stereotype: Avoid using or adopting ready-made, unoriginal expressions or opinions. It's reductive and can be harmful to the relevant communities.
4. Promote diversity: By including people from different cultural backgrounds in your thought process and decision-making, you'll already be taking a step forward in avoiding cultural appropriation.
5. Engage, promote and share benefits: Engaging with representatives from a culture other than your own can be extremely enriching and lead to all sorts of discoveries. It's

also a way to find out more about that culture and learn how to respect it.

Is There Any Legal Protection for Cultural Property?

In an attempt to reclaim cultural elements going back thousands of years and ensure the sustainability of their beliefs and cultural practices, Indigenous and minority communities around the world have tried to rethink intellectual property rights.

If we turn to copyright, protection is limited. With the exception of tangible creations from communities — such as pictorial, musical, sculptural and other works created by an individual and stored on physical media — there is no mechanism to protect a "culture."

At this point in time, no group of people can legally claim an artistic creation from its cultural heritage or history as their own. The Greeks, for example, can't claim any copyright on ancient Greek syllogism.

What's Next?

We're monitoring developments affecting cultural policy all over the world. UNESCO recently brought together 150 states for a three-day conference on that issue: MONDIACULT 2022.

It was an opportunity for the participating states to adopt a historic declaration affirming culture as a "global public good."

> The text defines a set of cultural rights that need to be taken into account in public policies, ranging from the social and economic rights of artists, to artistic freedom, the right of indigenous communities to safeguard and transmit their ancestral knowledge, and the protection and promotion of cultural and natural heritage.
>
> — UNESCO, MONDIACULT 2022: States adopt historic Declaration for Culture

VIEWPOINT 7

> "Copying is only a compliment. It's an acknowledgment from one human to another that, 'Hey, this is awesome. You're doing something right.'"

Cultural Appropriation Has Its Benefits
Steve Patterson

In this viewpoint, Steve Patterson argues that the debate around cultural appropriation is centered on abstractions rather than individual people. By this he means that it is based on the labels that are attached to people due to their race, gender, and other characteristics, many of which were set at birth. He argues that these labels dictate who can appreciate certain kinds of culture and who can't, which denies individuals agency over their preferences. He also argues that the concept of "culture" is glorified in a way that isn't accurate or helpful, that certain cultures possess unhelpful or downright toxic elements, and that it is in everyone's best interest to adopt the best aspects of the various cultures they're exposed to. Steve Patterson is the founder of the Natural Philosophy Institute and Dark Age Research Project.

As you read, consider the following questions:

1. What abstraction errors does Patterson argue are behind the outcry over cultural appropriation?

"Why Cultural Appropriation Is Actually A Good Thing," by Steve Patterson, Thought Catalog, November 24, 2015. Reprinted by permission.

2. What does Patterson mean when he writes that "cultures are not intrinsically valuable"?
3. Why does Patterson argue for individuals instead of abstractions?

Cultural criticism is taboo. In polite company, all cultures are created equally. None is better or worse than any other; they're just different. We aren't responsible for the culture we were born into, so there's no objective basis for criticism or judgement.

In progressive ideology, this idea goes a step further. Not only must we respect all cultural differences, we mustn't stray outside the norms of the culture we were born into. A white woman with dreadlocks, for example, should respect black culture and shave her hair off, rather than "steal" a hairstyle from a different culture. They even have a special word for this grievance: cultural appropriation.

I think cultural appropriation is a load of baloney, based on the most persistent errors in political/social thought: abstraction errors – misunderstanding the relationship between people and labels, between aggregates and concretes. These errors are not only imprecise, but they are counter-productive, divisive, and downright dangerous.

Equal Equivocation

The first abstraction error goes like this:

> All differences between people are benign differences. Some people are born with light hair; others with dark hair. Neither is superior to the other. In the same way, all cultural differences are benign. Some cultures value monogamy; others are more sexually liberal. Neither is superior to the other.

This concept is applied across the board. Some cultures are more religious; some value education more highly; some are more hierarchical, etc. These differences should not be judged, any more than we should judge somebody for their height or the amount of freckles on their face.

Then, the story goes, because all cultures are essentially equal, any differences in the socio-economic status of ethnic groups must be a function of discrimination. Without racism or discrimination, all cultures would be equally represented across the socio-economic spectrum.

In reality, we've no reason to believe this is true. Nowhere in the world – nowhere in history – are all cultures represented equally across the socio-economic spectrum. The idea is an appealing, aesthetic one, no doubt, but it's not grounded in the real world.

Different cultures value different things; some skills are valued more highly than others; throughout the world, Chinese immigrants tend to have the highest average income of any demographic. Why is this? It's not because they are genetically superior; it's not because of pro-Chinese discrimination (in fact, it's largely despite negative discrimination); it's because Chinese culture heavily emphasizes academic performance in the hard sciences, and the hard sciences tend to pay more than other fields.

But the purpose of this article isn't to explain the relationship between culture and economic status. I'll leave that to the fantastic work of Thomas Sowell. My point is to illustrate the concrete fact that some cultures are superior to others in specific ways.

Heritage Schmeritage

The second abstraction error goes like this: cultural heritage is intrinsically valuable. Preserving ethnic culture is an end by itself, regardless of the specifics. Progressives are especially fond of "indigenous cultures", that are assumed "pure" because they haven't been polluted by Western society. Whenever a new tribe of indigenous people is discovered, for example, progressives are adamant that we shouldn't disturb or influence their way of life – they want the complete preservation of cultures, the positive and the negative.

I have a radically different view. Cultures are not intrinsically valuable, nor should they be preserved by virtue of their uniqueness. Cultures emerge from different groups of people trying to best navigate the world. Sometimes, they do a good job. Other times, they do a bad job. If a bad cultural trait emerges, it should be destroyed and replaced – no different than bad theories about physics or mathematics.

In my mind, cultural "pride" is absurd. You are not responsible for the culture you're born into. There's nothing to be proud of. By happenstance of birth, you happen to have an ethnicity. It isn't superior or inferior to any other. You have nothing to defend or preserve. If you're fortunate, you'll be born into a positive culture. If you're unlucky, you'll be born into a toxic one.

For the sake of human progress, we should try to eliminate negative cultural values and promote positive ones. Saudi Arabian culture promotes beheadings for breaking the law – even for minor offenses. This is backwards, unnecessary, and a toxic cultural phenomenon. It shouldn't be preserved; it should be eliminated.

Group Identity

There's a fundamental abstraction error underlying all of this: group identity is inescapable. Individuals, in the progressive worldview, are seen as essentially tied to their ethnicity/socio-economic status. They are white men. Black women. Upper-class kids. They aren't "individuals with black skin" or "individuals with Scottish parents." The group identity is foundational; the individual is intrinsically a product of his environment and larger society.

You also see this phenomenon with progressives and their obsession with sexual orientation/gender labels. They self-identify first with their labels. They are fundamentally "lesbian," "transgender," or "cis-gender." All experiences are first filtered through the lenses they identify with – as if there's an entire category difference between humans with different sexual orientations.

I think this gets it backwards. Group identity is a label; it's a conceptual tool to more easily categorize people. It isn't foundational. The individual is the base-unit in society, and any labels we attach to them are secondary.

Practically speaking, the stronger people self-identify with labels, the more division it creates in society. "Class struggle" is a powerful idea, and it's entirely a function of group-identity. When you view people as individuals first, the differences between us seem minor and petty. I view my black neighbors as fundamentally peers. Not as aliens I can never relate to. They have a different daily experience than I do – as a function of their skin color – it's true. But it's not an essential difference, and it's absurd to obsess over it. We have far more in common than different.

Appropriate Appropriation

Put all the abstraction errors together, and you get the ultimate heresy: cultural appropriation – adopting some element from a culture outside your own. White people having "black hairstyles." Caucasians wearing Native American garb. Upper-class kids using inner-city slang.

Supposedly, cultural appropriation is insensitive. It trivializes the struggles and history of the culture being appropriated. Some people have even said, "Blues and rock'n'roll is 'black music.' If white people 'steal' it and make money, that's unfair!"

Ultimately, they are saying, "You are only allowed to behave in accordance with the culture into which you were born."

Again, it's abstractions first, individuals second. I find this idea preposterous and counter-productive. It's a tyranny of labels.

Based on the happenstance of your birth, progressives will assign you a list of approved behavior based on the genetics of your parents and grandparents. It's involuntary group membership with specific behavioral regulations.

And to what end? To preserve the divisions between people? To preserve different cultures for aesthetics' sake? It seems much more "progressive" to treat cultures like we do any other set of beliefs – we don't insist that "Islamic scientists refrain from doing American science" or "White philosophers only theorize about white philosophy."

I didn't choose my culture at birth, and I'll be damned if some progressive with a penchant for labels insists I must act in accordance with his list of "white, middle-class behavior." A few years ago, I moved to Atlanta, and there's always hip-hop and reggae music on the radio. I love it. I blast it when driving down the road. I also think afros look fantastic. If I had the hair for it, I would wear one myself. I also love soul food. The black culture in Atlanta has perfected fried chicken and collard greens (In fact, I ate some for lunch today).

Here's a healthy response to my love for blues music, soul food, and afros: it's wonderful. It helps bridge the gap between white and black people. Every individual is not only a consumer of culture, but a creator of culture. I want my behavior to incorporate the best of black culture, and hopefully the same is true in reverse.

It's an exciting idea: if you see everybody as individuals, then you'll see we're all trying to do the same thing in life. Different groups of people have discovered different truths, and why in the world wouldn't we want to share this knowledge with each other? We can, quite literally, take the best of all cultures and create something new and better.

How many black people discovered the game of golf through Tiger Woods? How many lives and careers have changed for the better because of it? It's a wonderful thing. How many white people have discovered rap through Eminem? I did, and it's a wonderful thing. We should celebrate cross-cultural exchanges of information, not lament them because the ambassador has an unapproved skin color.

The Flip Side

Of course, the same is true about the negative aspects of cultures. It's naïve to overlook cultural shortcomings because you don't want to offend people. From my experiences, I want to emulate parts of Chinese culture in terms of academic excellence. I don't want to emulate their emphasis on hierarchy. In my evaluation, Chinese parents can be too strict on their kids and are too focused on "family honor." So, I want to find a middle ground. Does that make me some anti-Chinese racist, because I recognize tendencies in that culture? Of course not.

I respect Chinese individuals enough to see positives and negatives in their culture, and I want the same treatment in return. The same is true for black culture, Hispanic culture, and every other group on the planet. There's absolutely no reason to take cultural norms as all-or-nothing. There's nothing to preserve for preservations' sake; let the positive live and the negative die.

For almost twenty years, I lived in an economically-depressed part of upstate New York. The culture was largely toxic and anti-intellectual. In terms of sorting the good from the bad, I'd say I'm leaving most of it behind.

My father was raised by a racist. My mother helped him see through the errors of racist ideas, and he raised all of his kids without an ounce of racist bias. That Southern racist culture died in my family, thanks to my parents, and I certainly will not resurrect it for my kids. This is progress and should be celebrated.

Imitation, Regulation, and Comingling

Before the fairly recent invention of intellectual property, artists took imitation and copying as a compliment. The myriad of "Variations on a Theme from Paganini" are all compliments to the wonderful work of the violinist Paganini. The same should apply to cultural phenomena.

Copying is only a compliment. It's an acknowledgment from one human to another that, "Hey, this is awesome. You're doing something right."

Versus, "Hey, you weren't born with the right ethnic membership to behave in this way. Stick to the white/black ways of doing things."

Instead, I think we should support cultures comingling with each other. Mix the genetics together, if you will, and see what offspring we can produce. If you like another culture's music, imitate it. If you like their fashion, wear it. The language, speak it. If you like how they raise their kids, then do the same. We'll all be better off.

Cultures are not delicate flowers that must be preserved until the end of time. They emerge from groups of people attempting to best navigate life. Some elements are good; others are bad. It's about time we grow up and recognize this. A lot of good will come from it.

Periodical and Internet Sources Bibliography

The following articles have been selected to supplement the diverse views presented in this chapter.

"Cultural Appreciation vs. Cultural Appropriation: Why It Matters," Greenheart Club. https://greenheart.org/blog/greenheart-international/cultural-appreciation-vs-cultural-appropriation-why-it-matters/.

Jenni Avins, "The Dos and Don'ts of Cultural Appropriation," the *Atlantic*. October 20, 2015. https://www.theatlantic.com/entertainment/archive/2015/10/the-dos-and-donts-of-cultural-appropriation/411292/.

Tina Charisma, "Cultural Appropriation vs. Cultural Appreciation: What's the Difference?," *Harper's Bazaar*, June 30, 2021. https://www.harpersbazaar.com/uk/culture/a36798089/cultural-appropriation-vs-cultural-appreciation/.

Emily Chen, Edric Huang, Jenny Dorsey, "Understanding…Cultural Appropriation," *Studio ATAO*, December 1, 2023. https://www.studioatao.org/cultural-appropriation.

George Chesterton, "Cultural Appropriation: Everything Is Culture and It's All Appropriated," *GQ*, September 1, 2020. https://www.gq-magazine.co.uk/article/the-trouble-with-cultural-appropriation.

Arlin Cuncic, "What Is Cultural Appropriation?" *VerywellMind*, November 8, 2022. https://www.verywellmind.com/what-is-cultural-appropriation-5070458.

Bel Jacobs, "What Defines Cultural Appropriation?," BBC, May 15, 2022. https://www.bbc.com/culture/article/20220513-what-defines-cultural-appropriation.

Nadra Kareem Nittle, "A Guide to Understanding and Avoiding Cultural Appropriation," *ThoughtCo*, February 4, 2021. https://www.thoughtco.com/cultural-appropriation-and-why-iits-wrong-2834561.

Dawnn Karen, "When Is It OK to Wear an Item from Another Culture, and When Is It Appropriation? How to Tell," Ideas.ted.com. https://ideas.ted.com/when-is-it-ok-to-wear-an-item-from-another-culture-and-when-is-it-appropriation-how-to-tell/.

Haley Lewis, "Indigenous Artists: It's OK to Buy, Wear Indigenous Art. Just Make Sure It's Authentic," *HuffPost*, September 28, 2018. https://www.huffpost.com/archive/ca/entry/indigenous-art-knockoffs-backlash.

Gloria Malone, "Cultural Conundrum: The Fine Line Between Appropriation and Homage," BELatina, April 1, 2019. https://belatina.com/cultural-conundrum-the-fine-line-between-appropriation-and-homage/.

Jordan Mendoza, "Is My Halloween Costume Offensive? What to Know About Cultural Appropriation," *USA Today*, October 25, 2021. https://www.usatoday.com/story/news/nation/2021/10/25/halloween-costumes-and-cultural-appropriation/6118430001/.

Lauren Moses, "Opinion: Cultural Appropriation Is a Joke," the *Daily Mississippian*, October 30, 2019. https://thedmonline.com/opinion-cultural-appropriation-is-a-joke/.

OPPOSING VIEWPOINTS® SERIES

CHAPTER 2

Is Cultural Appropriation a Problem in the Music Industry?

Chapter Preface

It would not be an exaggeration to say that the idea of cultural appropriation has been fueled and disseminated online. The internet has been a driving force in spreading ideas about who has the right to what culture and how they can use it. Like critical race theory, cultural appropriation was at first a purely academic concept, discussed in the dusty hallways of graduate schools, perhaps, but certainly not on the streets. The *Oxford English Dictionary* cites the earliest use of the phrase "cultural appropriation" as occurring in a 1945 essay by Arthur E. Christy on Orientalism. With the publication in 1976 of Kenneth Coutts-Smith's "Some General Observations on the Problems of Cultural Colonialism," the term became associated with a genre of academic theory known as post-colonial studies. But it never really took off outside of academia until the internet did the heavy lifting.

Perhaps this is one of the reasons why an all-white band from Brooklyn, New York, the Beastie Boys, never faced serious accusations of cultural appropriation. After all, these were three kids with Jewish backgrounds who affected a style drawn from Black culture and went on to fame and wealth as one of the most successful hip-hop acts of the late 20th century. Though a few rappers of their time took issue with the Beastie Boys' inauthenticity, there was no major outrage when, working with super producer Rick Rubin, their album *Licensed to Ill* became the first rap album to top the Billboard charts at number one. The very title of that hit record contains the Black slang word "ill," which means to be good at something. In effect, the Beastie Boys gave themselves license—or permission—to work within hip hop culture. It did not hurt that their record label, Def Jam, was cofounded by legendary Black producer Russell Simmons.

But the future may not be as kind to the Beastie Boys as the 1980s were. A 2022 essay by Rich Cromwell in the *Spectator* may well jump-start the re-evaluation of the band. "...the Beasties' entire career was an act of cultural appropriation," he writes.

Of course, it didn't hurt that the Beastie Boys were actually quite good at what they did, drawing legions of fans both Black and white. When white rapper Vanilla Ice (given name, Robert Matthew Van Winkle) tried to operate in the same space as the Beastie Boys, appropriating not only Black culture but a riff from Queen and David Bowie's "Under Pressure" and scoring a massive hit with "Ice, Ice Baby," he did not fare as well in public opinion. Nevertheless, this controversial figure gained the appreciation of many in the hip-hop world, including rapper Chuck D, who has said, "He broke through in the mid-South, in a Southern area in Texas, in something that was kind of indigenous to that hip-hop culture down there. He just doesn't get credit for it."

These examples suggest the fine line between accusations of cultural appropriation and praise for cultural appreciation. Essentially, cultural appropriation lives in the eye of the beholder. When Rich Cromwell writes that not only were the Beastie Boys masters of cultural appropriation, but "liberal New Yorkers just named an intersection after them," it may seem like pearl-clutching. Clearly those who named the intersection had no problem with the Beastie Boys' act.

But who knows? Perhaps someday the intersection will be renamed when 22nd century leaders erase and cancel the memory of any groups associated with cultural appropriation, in the same way that statues and street names dedicated to former slave owners and Confederate soldiers are being removed. After all, if two public schools in Berkeley, California, could remove the names of presidents (and slaveholders) George Washington and Thomas Jefferson, certainly white rappers, much less esteemed in the world, could be fair game. Perhaps the renowned Berklee School of Music in Boston, Massachusetts, will someday stop teaching their students the works of Lennon and McCartney, Jagger and Richards, Eric Clapton, and Elvis, all of whom were clearly guilty of cultural appropriation.

This is to say that we are now in a period where the internet rules, where everyone has a voice (for good or ill), and where offended parties have a platform to voice their opinions. For better or worse, it has pushed the discussion of cultural appropriation from the academic sphere to the public sphere.

VIEWPOINT 1

> "[Cultural appropriation is] a form of economic dominance and colonialism, of trying to establish or regain authority over a group of suppressed people."

Cultural Appropriation Is Widespread in the Music Industry

Parlé Magazine

This viewpoint provides a number of famous examples of cultural appropriation in the music industry to illustrate how widespread the practice has been. Examples from Cher to Miley Cyrus to Madonna are cited and discussed. While some of these artists have been properly respectful of their predecessors, many have blatantly confiscated elements from cultures without any sense of homage. The author addresses other musicians at the end of the viewpoint, urging them to conduct in-depth research and always show proper respect. Established in 2004, Parlé Magazine *began as an entertainment and lifestyle print publication distributed in New York City. The print publication featured some of the biggest names in music, literature, and film.*

As you read, consider the following questions:

1. How has globalization impacted cultural appropriation?

"7 Examples of Cultural Appropriation in Music," Parlé Magazine. Reprinted by permission. November 9, 2022.

2. Why, according to this viewpoint, was the Rolling Stones' use of Black blues music somewhat less offensive than other examples of the practice?
3. What advice does the viewpoint offer to prospective musicians?

Humans have been nurturing their cultures for millennia and consider them something precious. However, it is impossible to protect them from external influence. Nor can nations prevent other people from borrowing or stealing their cultural treasures.

The phrase "cultural appropriation" has been around for quite some time, particularly in the music industry. Though you might not be familiar with its exact meaning, you've probably come across several examples. For instance, Elvis Presley rocked and rolled (considered black music at the time) to pave his path to stardom.

With globalization, it's become easier to appropriate other cultures. Artists 'borrow' elements and use them to entertain the masses or for lucrative purposes. Here are some examples of famous musicians who relied heavily on cultural appropriation in music.

What Is Cultural Appropriation?

Adopting elements from one culture by someone with a different background is known as cultural appropriation. This practice usually happens when a dominant community appropriates the culture of a disadvantaged minority and exploits it for financial and commercial gains. In order to understand the notion, one should look through cultural appropriation essays that dwell upon it extensively. They provide plenty of examples when certain people have used the heritage of other cultures for their own or their community's benefit.

As a result, the subjugated cultures lose their traits without receiving due credit, respect, or compensation. In 2018, the term cultural appropriation entered the Oxford English Dictionary. In short, it means unacknowledged and improper adoption of the customs and traditions of a social or ethnic group by members of a dominant society. Hence, it's a form of economic dominance and colonialism, of trying to establish or regain authority over a group of suppressed people.

Madonna

Topping the list, this pop star has Italian and American roots. However, Madonna's origin didn't stop her from borrowing elements from several cultures. In an attempt to commercialize and sell her music, Madonna is someone who borrowed features from the Black, Indian, Latin American, and gay cultures.

The superstar used to wear Indian garments like saris and bindis for photography sessions. She also took part in a geisha-inspired photo shoot. Finally, considering her massive hits "La Isla Bonita" and "Vogue," one can see how much they hold onto Latin American music and gay and Black cultures, respectively.

Perhaps one positive aspect of Madonna's cultural appropriation is that she has given underrepresented communities wider exposure. Yet she has never made any political or cultural statements. Hence, many believe that her use of cultural artifacts is superficial.

"Tumbling Dice" by the Rolling Stones, 1972

The world-class band owes a lot of its fame to the blues genre. Even their name originated from the song "Rollin' Stone" by Muddy Waters, one of the most influential rock' n' roll artists. Indeed, the British band wasn't very creative before they became famous. They emulated R&B artists and recorded covers for songs like "Down in the Bottom."

However, the Rolling Stones admired jazz and African-American blues openly. They never tried to borrow cultural elements without speaking about them or giving proper credit. Their model of appropriation is acceptable in a way because of the conscious tribute.

"D'Yer Mak'er" by Led Zeppelin, 1973

In the early 1970s, Bob Marley was already an established household name. The aspiring band Led Zeppelin also wanted to jump on the sweet reggae bandwagon. So what did they do? They recorded a reggae-inspired song under a title from a Cockney joke. In fact, "D'Yer Mak'er" is a play on the word Jamaica pronounced with an English accent.

Rolling Stone claimed that the song represents a pathetic attempt at reggae and that Zeppelin was laughing off the island of Jamaica. Overall, the band demonstrated little understanding of the essence of reggae, and their song lacked fundamental reggae features. Considering the title, the band showed gross insensitivity towards Jamaican culture.

Cher's "Half-Breed"

Another example of popular culture borrowing elements from Native Americans is Cher's single "Half-Breed" because the term is offensive to that community. However, in 1973 things were different, and a White artist could get away with sexing up Native American culture and garments.

In the song, Cher shares a story that isn't hers. She highlights the dilemma faced by half-White and half-Cherokee young women. Still, critics don't approve of how she turned Native American cultural elements into a costume. Cher was ignorant of the comments and continued to perform the song on stage.

Miley Cyrus and Hip-Hop Culture

Miley Cyrus became renowned for the show Hannah Montana in Disney Production. As a child, she portrayed a different image of herself in public, so everyone knew her as the sweet little rich girl. Yet, she suddenly decided to change her ways and do something more urban.

Miley wanted her songs to feel black and not fairytale-like. Her single "We Can't Stop" refers to substance use, and she debuts an "urban" appearance. Cyrus even co-performed with rapper Juicy

J in Los Angeles. The crowds were perplexed to see her feature gold teeth and twerk. But twerking wasn't her invention (it existed long before), and the public heavily criticized Miley for using Black culture to build her career.

Trap Music

The trap genre is a hip-hop variant originating from the Southern parts of the US. It features a heavy bass rhythm and deals with issues of people from a lower socio-economic status. More specifically, the lyrics speak of crime, drug dealing, and other ghetto problems of "trapped" people.

Though trap music dates back to the '90s, the latest songs contain no lyrics and are mostly performed by White people. This appropriation steals the essence of the genre. US ghettos lose their central position, and the roots of trap music may soon get obliterated.

Iggy Azalea

White people can rap, and Eminem is an incredible specimen of this ability. The problem arises when some White artists aren't authentic and mimic a Black vocal style. Iggy Azalea is one such example. While she had a remarkable reputation at the onset, she ruined it by transforming herself into something she wasn't.

Iggy banished her Australian accent and started rapping with "blaccent," which is offensive. The masses recognized this and weren't in favor of it, but Azalea dismissed the accusations of cultural appropriation. She picked various Black cultural elements without giving credit.

Wrap-Up

The benefits of using elements from cultures other than yours are short-term. So, if you're new in the music industry and planning to build your career on stable grounds, refrain from this practice. However, some artists reach for other cultures once they become famous, only to boost their financial gain.

Pop Music Is the Monetization of Black Music

As long as popular culture has existed in western society, the appropriation and monetization of Black culture has been a persistent issue that seems to go unheard of, or if talked about, never cared for enough. Despite the recently increasing amount of activism towards the appropriation of Black culture, the whitewashing of Black music that's been happening for decades upon decades is an issue that goes beyond appropriation or "borrowing" from Black culture.

One of the most infamous examples of Black music being stolen and profited off of by an industry and audience favoring white artists is the emergence of rock: case in point, Elvis Presley. Despite Presley being considered the "King of Rock," Black rock n' roll artists such as Chuck Berry and Little Richard were majorly influential to his music, to the point where he would perform and release the same songs that were originally performed by Black artists.

The difference was that Presley's status, privilege, and race gave him the upper hand and the ability to popularize the genre to the public. With more and more white rock artists emerging after Presley, whether they acknowledged their influences and the source of rock music or not, the genre as a whole now had a white face on it. As a result, rock is being labeled and generalized as white culture to the point where it's now been stereotyped as "white middle-class" music.

Instances such as these show how Black culture is stolen and marketed to the general audience by a lighter-skinned image, since it's more accepted by the general audience. Whether white artists give credit to the Black artists and musicians that influenced them, the music industry sweeps their work and influence under the rug. The underrepresentation and oppression of Black and POC minority groups goes much further than social interactions or microaggressions; it's embedded in the pop culture and media everyone consumes. The appropriation of Black culture has become the norm without us even noticing.

[…]

"'Pop Music is Black Music' – The Cultural Appropriation (and monetization) of Black Music," by Evan Ochoa, The Communicator, October 7, 2022.

Cultural Appropriation

But even then, fans can label you racist and disrespectful of others. Finally, if you insist on using a segment from a culture you like, research it first to see if it fits your style and music, and always pay respect.

VIEWPOINT 2

> "Cultural appropriation is both enabled by power and is an expression of power."

South African Band Die Antwoord's Success Is a Blatant Example of Cultural Appropriation

Adam Haupt

In this viewpoint Adam Haupt discusses how the South African hip-hop band Die Antwoord (which translates as "The Answer") appropriated Black culture in order to achieve worldwide fame. Taking their cue from Black South Africans who rapped in the Kaaps language, and mimicking the style of local gang members, the two founding members of Die Antwoord, neither of whom were Black nor impoverished, created a band that is virtually the definition of cultural appropriation. Haupt considers their act to be a modern form of blackface, in which they adopt, adapt, and caricature South African Black culture. As opposed to the originators of the music they have appropriated, they and their corporate backers have the power to gain global fame at the expense of impoverished minorities back in their homeland. Adam Haupt is director of the Centre for Film and Media Studies at the University of Cape Town in South Africa.

"What is cultural appropriation and why is it so harmful?," by Adam Haupt, The Conversation, October 9, 2022. https://theconversation.com/what-is-cultural-appropriation-and-why-is-it-so-harmful-185976. Licensed under CC BY-ND 4.0 International.

Cultural Appropriation

As you read, consider the following questions:

1. How has the band Die Antwoord appropriated the language and culture of more disadvantaged South Africans?
2. According to the viewpoint, how does the notion of power factor into the success of their act?
3. In what specific ways does Haupt draw a parallel between Die Antwoord's act and the now largely taboo (at least in the U.S.) tradition of blackface?

Die Antwoord is a South African band that uses hip-hop music to create a style it calls "zef." Since it first appeared in 2009, Die Antwoord has been criticised for cultural appropriation (using cultural elements of a minority group in an exploitative way). It's accused of copying the lyrics and styles of Cape Town artists rapping in South Africa's Kaaps language, and of mimicking the visual styles of Cape Flats gang members. Adam Haupt has researched and written extensively on hip-hop and identity. He discusses cultural appropriation and the role of power in interactions between dominant and marginalised subjects in a case like Die Antwoord's.

What Is Cultural Appropriation?

In an article on cultural appropriation, visual culture scholar Rina Arya writes:

> Integral to the definition of cultural appropriation is an asymmetry of power between two cultures that involves the majority/dominant culture taking from the marginalised culture.

So, it's more productive to think about cultural appropriation in terms of relations of power. For example, in South Africa, Afrikaner nationalists appropriated the local Kaaps language to produce the Afrikaans language, a version that stripped Kaaps of its creolised Khoi San, Arabic and south-east Asian roots to favour its Dutch origins because it could do so.

Cultural appropriation is both enabled by power and is an expression of power.

How Is Die Antwoord a Good Example of This?

Die Antwoord means "the answer" in Afrikaans, the language associated with the dominant white minority rulers of apartheid South Africa.

The band has two members, Ninja and Yolandi. They created a hip hop outfit using Kaaps as a basis for their lyrics and styling Ninja as a Cape Town gangster. So, a privileged white man, Waddy Jones, created Ninja after previously crafting other hip hop personas such as Max Normal. Jones is neither "black"/"coloured" nor "white" working-class. He is not a gangster either.

Stereotypically, speakers of Kaaps have been presented as "mixed race" or "coloured" people. They were segregated from other categories of black South Africans in the service of apartheid ideology. Speakers of Kaaps have also been denigrated as speakers of "slang", as if Kaaps were not a language in its own right.

To become known, Die Antwoord employed social media alongside performances at music festivals. The cartoonish violence and phallic imagery in its first video, Enter the Ninja, was designed to go viral. Once it did, the band was soon able to perform extensively in Europe and the US, thanks to a record deal.

In my book *Static: Race and Representation in Post-Apartheid Music and Media*, I argue that Die Antwoord's success is thanks in part to racialised class inequality in South Africa and the fact that systemic racism has yet to be dismantled nearly three decades after democracy. The band used class privilege, social capital and networks to ensure that it succeeded – often at the expense of marginalised communities.

How Did the Cultural Appropriation Work?

Die Antwoord "borrows" heavily from Kaaps (also known as Afrikaaps) and from Afrikaans hip-hop. It draws on words and cultural expressions associated with black/coloured and white working-class multilingual speech communities. So it piggybacked off work done by black artists who established the cool of "rapping in the vernac".

Die Antwoord could appropriate this music because it had the power to do so. But its appropriation went beyond performing verbal stereotypes. It was also embodied, for example, in Ninja adorning his body with particular Cape gang tattoos. To quote *Static:*

> The band alludes to the numbers gangs, the 26s and 28s, via tattoos and the graffiti that appears in the background of their set.

Die Antwoord then sold itself as authentically South African to a global audience that knew nothing of the culture being appropriated.

Who Actually Pioneered Afrikaans Hip Hop?

Afrikaans/Kaaps hip hop was initially pioneered by the groups Prophets of da City and Brasse Vannie Kaap in the 1990s. It is now also championed by a wide range of hip hop artists from the Western Cape province, such as Rosey die Rapper, YoungstaCPT, Emile YX? and Jitsvinger to name just a few.

Prophets and Brasse did a great deal to validate black multilingualism in an environment that still favoured imperial language. Members of Prophets of da City went on to form bands like Skeem and Boom Shaka, shaping the country's youthful kwaito music revolution. Kwaito affirms black multilingual modes of speech.

Where Does Blackface Fit In?

While we might argue Die Antwoord's use of tattoos and oblique references to the numbers gangs is a form of blackface, band members have literally blackened their bodies in the music video for the song Fatty Boom Boom, for example. Die Antwoord proudly displays blackface as part of its persona.

Cultural Appropriation and Appreciation in Music

Artists are crossing cultural lines with music, as evidenced by recent Billboard Hot 100 hits like Post Malone's "Wow.," Ariana Grande's "7 rings" and Cardi B and Bruno Mars' "Please Me."

But when they break these boundaries and take on genres from other cultures, some fans wonder if artists are practicing cultural appreciation or cultural appropriation.

Cultural appropriation is when a person takes elements from another culture without paying tribute to their authenticity and value, said Timothy Welbeck, an Africology and African American Studies instructor.

Post Malone, Ariana Grande, Bruno Mars and Iggy Azalea, all non-Black artists, are known for performing music like R&B and hip-hop influenced by Black people and culture.

Azalea's performances, particularly the voice she uses while rapping, is an example of appropriation, Welbeck said. Azalea uses a "blaccent," an imitation of a Black accent by a non-Black person, while rapping, he added.

"When she raps, she sounded like a poor imitation of a Black woman who lived in an urban area in America," Welbeck said. "But then when she spoke, she spoke in a dignified Australian accent."

When an artist tries to profit from the music style without showing respect to the culture, they also demonstrate cultural appropriation, said Gabriella Duran, a freshman global studies and political science major.

Justin Bieber's inclusion on the remix of "Despacito" stood out to Duran as a bilingual track that disrespected Spanish culture and helped Bieber profit.

"Music is an art form, and we can learn so much from it when it's done correctly," Duran said.

But distinguishing between cultural appreciation and appropriation in music isn't always easy to define. Fans of Bruno Mars debated whether or not the artist respectfully represented Black culture in his music last March, Vice reported.

Mars was accused of cultural appropriation by Seren Sensei, a writer and activist, but Black celebrities defended him on Twitter.

continued on next spread

> Sensei accused Mars of using "his racial ambiguity to cross genres." In response, celebrities tweeted he has paid homage to Black culture and helped bring back certain aspects of the culture's sound.
> Mars, whose father is Puerto Rican and Jewish and mother is Filipina, often credits Michael Jackson and other Black musicians as inspirations.
> "The situation is complicated, but the point is that there is a lot of misunderstandings and not enough conversation," said Dynas Johnson, a junior English major.
> [...]
>
> "How to separate cultural appreciation, appropriation in music," by Michelle Mendez, The Temple News, November 22, 2022.

The US cultural historian Eric Lott reveals that blackface minstrelsy took shape in the US in the 1800s when "white men caricatured 'blacks' for sport and profit" by painting their own faces black and performing racist caricatures of "black" subjects for "white" audiences. These projections of blackness had little to do with the lived experiences of "black" subjects.

The US historian Alexander Saxton contends that minstrel shows "merged into vaudeville and the beginnings of cinema."

Blackface is not a thing of the past. We need only think of South African filmmaker Leon Schuster's many blackface performances in comedy movies that continue to appeal to South African audiences. Who can forget US singer Miley Cyrus twerking or the Dutch continuing to defend their blackface Christmas tradition Zwarte Piet as "traditional"?

Cultural appropriation and blackface persists in popular culture in a world facing a resurgence of right wing politics in the form of ethnonationalism, xenophobia and fascism. To this day, black communities fight for the right to represent themselves on their own terms with dignity.

Die Antwoord's use of cultural appropriation to gain global fame is enabled by the continuing asymmetry of power relations that play out along race, gender and class lines.

VIEWPOINT 3

> "I can't help but think of it as basically every big pop musician looks with a sense of - how do I engage with another culture that my brand is pretty removed from? And they almost always botch it."

Cultural Appropriation Has Been the Norm in Pop Music
Rachel Martin

In this viewpoint, Rachel Martin and Justin Charity discuss the proliferation of new music that engages with another culture in ways that are offensive to some and, at best, merely inappropriate. From Coldplay and Beyonce to Iggy Azalea and Madonna, artists have been crossing cultural boundaries for many years, but, as Charity states, they often err in doing so. The line between a superficial indulgence and true interest in another's culture is a fine one. But, as Martin observes, the phenomenon of musical cultural appreciation seems to work on some level, at least for the artists, the record companies, and many of the artist's fans. Rachel Martin is a founding host of NPR's award-winning morning news podcast "Up First."

©2016 National Public Radio, Inc. NPR news report titled "Cultural Appropriation In Pop Music — When Are Artists In the Wrong?" by Rachel Martin was originally published on npr.org on February 7, 2016, and is used with the permission of NPR. Any unauthorized duplication is strictly prohibited.

Cultural Appropriation

As you read, consider the following questions:

1. How did the Coldplay and Beyonce music video cross the line for some people?
2. What, according to the viewpoint, is the key element that can remove accusations of cultural appropriation by musical artists?
3. Why, according to Charity, do pop musicians continue to use a formula that is offensive to some?

When Coldplay and Beyoncé released the music video for their new song, they were immediately accused of cultural appropriation. What does that mean? And how pervasive is it in the music industry?

RACHEL MARTIN, HOST: This is WEEKEND EDITION from NPR News. I'm Rachel Martin. The Super Bowl halftime usually features the biggest names in music. Today will be no different with Coldplay and Beyonce on stage. They will not, however, be performing their new song, "Hymn For The Weekend." The music video for the song dropped last week.

(SOUNDBITE OF SONG, "HYMN FOR THE WEEKEND")

COLDPLAY AND BEYONCE: (Singing) Oh, angel sent from up above. You know you make my world light up.

MARTIN: And then the headlines followed. Here's one of them. Dear Coldplay and Beyonce, India is not an Orientalist fantasy. Coldplay has said they're not performing the song because it's, quote, "too new."

Whatever the reason, the controversy around "Hymn For The Weekend" has continued, so we called up Justin Charity. He's a staff writer at the magazine *Complex*. And I asked him first off to just describe the video.

JUSTIN CHARITY: Basically, Coldplay and Beyonce went to Mumbai, and the music video is shot with a lot of imagery from the Hindu Holi festival of colors. The music video features Chris Martin running around with local children and sort of throwing dry coloring and dye. And Beyonce's also in it, and she is basically a Bollywood actress. And she's adorned in lace and bangles and henna, and this is all somewhat strange imagery to associate with either Beyonce or Coldplay.

MARTIN: Neither of them are Indian.

CHARITY: Right. We should note that Chris Martin is a white man.

MARTIN: (Laughter).

CHARITY: Beyonce is a black woman from Houston, Texas.

MARTIN: So what does this mean? It means if you're an artist, you are only allowed to operate in an artistic space that reflects your own ethnic identity?

CHARITY: I don't think that that's necessarily the complaint about the song - right? - because Chris Martin has talked about writing "Hymn For The Weekend," and he was hearing a Flo Rida song, and he thought, I really want to write a club hit. So to go from Chris Martin hearing a Flo Rida pop rap record to Chris Martin and Beyonce being in Mumbai is a strange cultural leap that seems like it's basically appropriating a very distant culture that the music video's not really engaging with as this sort of visual aesthetic for what is ultimately Coldplay trying to do a Flo Rida song (laughter).

MARTIN: So you're saying it's different if the song had some resonance, some direct connection to South Asia or to these traditions.

Cultural Appropriation

CHARITY: Right, and if the song or the video seemed at all curious about its surrounding, which it doesn't, you know. I can't help but think of it as basically every big pop musician looks with a sense of - how do I engage with another culture that my brand is pretty removed from? And they almost always botch it.

MARTIN: So, you know, it's hard to have a conversation about cultural appropriation without bringing up Iggy Azalea.

CHARITY: Iggy Azalea has been in this territory with the music video for "Bounce," I believe, which also is basically appropriating a Bollywood aesthetic for the sake of a white Australian rapper who is doing a strange approximation of Atlanta rap music. So it's even stranger in Iggy's case, right?

MARTIN: And Miley and the twerking?

CHARITY: Well, that's the thing. It's, like, you can talk about Miley and twerking. We can talk about Gwen Stefani - I think, like, 12 years ago in the Harajuku Girls controversy.

MARTIN: Yeah. Madonna even did this stuff in the '90s.

CHARITY: Right. Right (laughter).

MARTIN: So, why does it keep happening? Something about that formula works to some degree.

CHARITY: I think it's more about the fact that this is what pop culture does. You know, you can look to the fact that in the late '90s and beyond, like, hip-hop went from being a very New York-local genre of music to being a multimillion dollar industry that profited a lot of people beyond just the artisan producers involved in the creation of the music, right? That's sort of the M.O. of pop music. That's the M.O. of record labels. That's the M.O. of artists

Is Cultural Appropriation a Problem in the Music Industry?

once they engage with pop culture on a certain level, is to find ways to commodify imagery that's interesting to people, even if that imagery is interesting to consumers at a great distance.

MARTIN: Justin Charity writes for *Complex*. Thanks so much, Justin.

CHARITY: Thank you, Rachel.

(SOUNDBITE OF SONG, "HYMN FOR THE WEEKEND")

COLDPLAY AND BEYONCE: (Singing) Ah, ah-ah, ah-ah, la, la, la, la, la, la, la...

VIEWPOINT 4

> "He wanted to fold the era's popular jazz music into classical music—and, in doing so, draw out the inherent beauty in the beast, making it more acceptable to white audiences."

The Work of George Gershwin Shows that the Question of Cultural Appropriation in Music Is Not New

Ryan Raul Bañagale

In this viewpoint, Ryan Raul Bañagale explains the process of composing George Gershwin's 1924 hit "Rhapsody in Blue," how the musical composition was received by white audiences and Black musicians, and the enduring legacy of the piece. Gershwin—who was a Jewish-American composer—drew heavily on the work of Black jazz musicians in composing this piece. Even at that time—well before the term "cultural appropriation" was being used—Black musicians did not appreciate having their music pilfered. Gershwin argued that his composition was a musical version of America's melting pot, but others argue that it simply provides a "sanitized" version of jazz, a traditionally Black genre, for white audiences. Ryan Raul Bañagale is an associate professor and chair of music at Colorado College.

"George Gershwin's 'Rhapsody in Blue' Is a Story of Jazz, Race and the Fraught Notion of America's Melting Pot," by Ryan Raul Bañagale, February 7, 2024, The Conversation, https://theconversation.com/george-gershwins-rhapsody-in-blue-is-a-story-of-jazz-race-and-the-fraught-notion-of-americas-melting-pot-213058. Licensed under CC BY-ND 4.0 International.

Is Cultural Appropriation a Problem in the Music Industry?

As you read, consider the following questions:

1. According to this viewpoint, what were some of the influences for George Gershwin's "Rhapsody in Blue"?
2. What does Bañagale argue is the problem with the "melting pot" metaphor?
3. According to this viewpoint, what is the origin of the terms "highbrow" and "lowbrow"? Why is this problematic?

February 12, 1924, was a frigid day in New York City. But that didn't stop an intrepid group of concertgoers from gathering in midtown Manhattan's Aeolian Hall for "An Experiment in Modern Music." The organizer, bandleader Paul Whiteman, wanted to show how jazz and classical music could come together. So he commissioned a new work by a 25-year-old Jewish-American upstart named George Gershwin.

Gershwin's contribution to the program, "Rhapsody in Blue," would go on to exceed anyone's wildest expectations, becoming one of the best-known works of the 20th century. Beyond the concert hall, it would appear in iconic films such as Woody Allen's "Manhattan" and Disney's "Fantasia 2000." It was performed during the opening ceremonies of the 1984 Los Angeles Olympics, and if you ever fly on United Airlines, you'll hear it playing during the preflight safety videos.

I've spent nearly two decades researching and writing about this piece. To me, "Rhapsody" isn't some static composition stuck in the past; rather, it's a continuously evolving piece of music whose meaning has changed over time.

Programming "Rhapsody" for concerts today has become somewhat of a double-edged sword. A century after it premiered, it remains a crowd favorite – and almost always guarantees a sold-out show. But more and more scholars are starting to see the work as a whitewashed version of Harlem's vibrant Black music scene.

A Cobbled-Together Hit

Whiteman commissioned Gershwin to write "Rhapsody" sometime in late 1923. But as the story goes, the composer forgot about his assignment until he read about the upcoming concert in a newspaper on Jan. 4, 1924.

Gershwin had to work quickly, writing as time allowed in his busy schedule. Manuscript evidence suggests that he only worked on the piece a total of 10 days over the span of several weeks.

Accordingly, he relied on the familiar melodies, harmonies, rhythms and musical structures that had started to garner him acclaim as a popular composer for the Broadway stage. This music was increasingly influenced by early jazz, as the improvised, syncopated and blues-infused sound of Black musicians such as Louis Armstrong made its way north from New Orleans. Gershwin also mingled with, and was influenced by, some of the great Harlem stride pianists of the day, including James P. Johnson and Willie "The Lion" Smith.

Despite being quickly cobbled together, "Rhapsody in Blue" ultimately sold hundreds of thousands of records and copies of sheet music. Gershwin's own performances of the work on tour also helped boost its popularity.

But success also opened up the piece to criticism – particularly that Gershwin had appropriated Black music.

Black Musicians Feel Snubbed

This is not only a 21st-century critique by music historians. Even back then, some Black artists were miffed.

But rather than calling it out in print, they did so through their own art.

In 1929, blues artist Bessie Smith starred in a short film called "St. Louis Blues," based on the song of the same name by composer W.C. Handy. It features an all-Black cast, including members of the Fletcher Henderson Orchestra and the Hall Johnson Choir. Instrumental and vocal versions of Handy's song provide the sonic backdrop for this 15-minute film – with one very pointed exception.

Smith plays the part of Bessie, an unrequited lover to a duplicitous gambler named Jimmy. In the final scene, after a previous falling out, Jimmy and Bessie reconcile in a club. They embrace on the dance floor to the strains of "St. Louis Blues."

But unbeknownst to the love-struck Bessie, Jimmy carefully picks her pocket and unmercifully shoves her back to her bar stool. After Jimmy flashes his newly acquired bankroll, the opening clarinet glissando of "Rhapsody in Blue" begins. During this brief, 20-second cue, Jimmy boastfully backs out of the club, bowing and tipping his hat like a performer acknowledging his ovation.

It's hard not to see the subtext of introducing Gershwin's famous piece at this moment: Just as Jimmy has robbed Bessie, the film suggests that Gershwin had pilfered jazz from the Black community.

Another musical response to "Rhapsody" emerged in 1927 from Gershwin's stride pianist friend, James P. Johnson: "Yamekraw." Publisher Perry Bradford billed the work as "not a 'Rhapsody in Blue,' but a Rhapsody in Black and White (Black notes on White paper)."

Of course, the "black notes" were more than just the score itself. Johnson demonstrates how a Black musician would approach the rhapsody genre.

Stuck in the Middle with 'Blue'

Gershwin once described "Rhapsody" "as a sort of musical kaleidoscope of America – of our vast melting pot."

The problem with the "melting pot" metaphor is that it asks immigrants to leave behind cultural practices and identities in order to assimilate into the majority population.

And that's just what Whiteman's musical experiment at Aeolian Hall a century ago was all about: He sought, as he put it, to "make a lady out of jazz."

As the concert's program read, "Mr. Whiteman intends to point out, with the assistance of his orchestra and associates, the tremendous strides which have been made in popular music from the day of the discordant Jazz … to the really melodious music of today."

In other words, he wanted to fold the era's popular jazz music into classical music – and, in doing so, draw out the inherent beauty in the beast, making it more acceptable to white audiences.

"Rhapsody in Blue" and other classical-jazz hybrid works like it would soon become known as "middlebrow" music.

This fraught term emerges from the space between the so-called "lowbrow" and "highbrow," descriptors that locate works of art on a scale from pedestrian to intellectual. These terms originally related to the pseudoscience of phrenology, which drew conclusions about intelligence based on skull shape and the location of the ridge of one's brow line.

Highbrow music, made by and for white people, was considered the most sophisticated.

But highbrow music could also conveniently elevate lowbrow music by borrowing – or rather, appropriating – musical elements such as rhythm and harmony. Merging the two, the low gets to the middle. But it could never get to the top on its own terms.

If Gershwin's "Rhapsody" is meant to be heard as a "musical kaleidoscope of America," it is important to remember who's holding the lens, what music gets added to the mix, and how it has changed once admitted.

But it's also important to remember that 100 years is a long time. What the culture values, and why, inevitably changes. The same is true for "Rhapsody in Blue."

Periodical and Internet Sources Bibliography

The following articles have been selected to supplement the diverse views presented in this chapter.

Marcella Barneclo, "Dear Music Industry, Culture Does Not Exist for Your Profit," *Guardian UCSD*, April 18, 2021. https://ucsdguardian.org/2021/04/18/dear-music-industry-culture-does-not-exist-for-your-profit/.

Elizabeth De Luna, "'They Use Our Culture': The Black Creatives and Fans Holding K-pop Accountable," *Guardian*, July 20, 2021. https://www.theguardian.com/music/2020/jul/20/k-pop-black-fans-creatives-industry-accountable-race.

Ruka Hatua-Saar White, "Cultural Appropriation in Music," Berklee Online. https://online.berklee.edu/takenote/cultural-appropriation-in-music/.

Chris Jancelewicz, "The 'Whitewashing' of Black Music: A Dark Chapter in Rock History," *Global News*, July 30, 2019. https://globalnews.ca/news/4321150/black-music-whitewashing-classic-rock/.

Nadra Kareem Nittle, "Cultural Appropriation in Music: From Madonna to Miley Cyrus," ThoughtCo., December 14, 2020. https://www.thoughtco.com/cultural-appropriation-in-music-2834650.

Peter L. Manuel, "Musical Borrowings, Copyright, and the Canard of 'Cultural Appropriation,'" CUNY Academic Works, 2021. https://academicworks.cuny.edu/cgi/viewcontent.cgi?article=1543&context=jj_pubs.

John McWhorter, "You Can't 'Steal' a Culture: In Defense of Cultural Appropriation," *Daily Beast*, April 14, 2017. https://www.thedailybeast.com/you-cant-steal-a-culture-in-defense-of-cultural-appropriation.

Michele Mendez, "How to Separate Cultural Appreciation, Appropriation in Music," *Temple News*, April 9, 2019. https://temple-news.com/music-cultural-appreciation-or-appropriation/.

Arun Starkey, "The Whitewashing of Black Music: Five Singles Made Popular by WhiteArtists," *Far Out Magazine*, August 11, 2021.

https://faroutmagazine.co.uk/the-whitewashing-of-black-music-five-singles-made-popular-by-white-artists/.

Brittni Williams, "5 Non-Black Artists Who Appreciate — Not Appropriate — Black Culture," *21Ninety*, January 11, 2023. https://www.21ninety.com/artists-who-appreciate-black-culture.

L.T. Wright, "Did White People Really Steal Rock Music from Black People?" *Hub Pages*, August 20, 2020. https://discover.hubpages.com/entertainment/did-white-people-steal-rock-music.

CHAPTER 3

Is Cultural Appropriation a Problem in the Film Industry?

Chapter Preface

Was Disney's original portrayal of Mickey Mouse racist? Was it an example of culturally inappropriate blackface? The question might almost sound absurd, and yet it has been stirring up the internet for years. In his book, *Birth of An Industry: Blackface Minstrelsy and the Rise of American Animation*, Nicholas Sammond, who teaches Cinema Studies at the University of Toronto, argues that many of the conventions of blackface are actually hiding in plain sight. For example, in that icon of Americana, Mickey Mouse. According to Sammond,

> His facial characteristics, the gloves he sometimes wears, the way that he acts, his bodily plasticity, his ability to take punishment all are kind of markers of the minstrel that are actually—had—were kind of established by the time he came on the scene in the late 1920s.

This is certainly a disturbing revelation, considering that Mickey Mouse is one of America's most beloved characters. But is it definitively true that the cartoon was based on negative and stereotypical tropes? The answer, as usual, is somewhat complicated.

For a long time now cinema buffs have debated whether Walt Disney was racist or anti-Semitic. Undoubtedly some of his early films, such as *Song of the South,* are highly controversial for racist depictions, so much so that the 1946 film was never released for home purchase in the U.S. Some have also argued that Disney's 1933 film *Three Little Pigs* perpetuated anti-Semitic tropes.

One has to look no further than the infamous crow sequence in *Dumbo* or the monkeys in the *Jungle Book* to find depictions that are uncomfortable at best and racist at worst (though both scenes have their apologists and defenders in the cinematic world). Here's how *Washington Post* reporter Travis M. Andrews characterizes the crow scene in *Dumbo*:

Perhaps the most famously decried scene from the original arrives when Dumbo meets a group of crows. The black birds are depicted using African American stereotypes of the time, with jive-like speech patterns and jazzy-gospely songs sung in harmony. The main bird, named Jim Crow, was voiced by white actor Cliff Edwards, who engages in the vocal equivalent of blackface.

Despite scenes such as this one, some recent studies have disputed whether Mickey Mouse as well was truly based on racist tropes. For example, a 2023 study by Çağdaş Ülgen titled "Blackface Makeup and Mickey Mouse Character in the Context of Racism and Discrimination," questions whether Disney's most famous creation actually owes to racist tropes. While admitting that caricatures of Black people were common enough in the early 20th century, Ülgen finds that many of the design elements for early depictions of Mickey Mouse were based more on practical measures than racial insensitivity.

When it comes to Mickey Mouse's exaggerated movements and body plasticity, for example, Ülgen suggests that awkwardly moving buffoons and fools are comedic tropes in works dating back to ancient civilizations, from Egypt and Greece through Shakespeare all the way up to Charlie Chaplin, Buster Keaton, and the Three Stooges. As for Mickey's black body, Ülgen sees this as a practical choice: it stands out best on a white background. "In the early period of cartoons," Ülgen writes, "it was a necessity to design the characters in black and white, since color films had not yet been invented." So, too, are Mickey's white gloves a practical measure to display his hands better against his black body.

All of this is not to say that racial tropes may not have played a part in designing Mickey Mouse. But perhaps, as Ülgen sees it, the matter is not as cut and dried as some may believe. What we do know is that the history of cultural appropriation in cinema is a long and sorry one, and that white characters in blackface played a role in many early films, just as white actors played Asians, Native Americans, and other people of color.

But in the 21st century, Hollywood seems well on its way toward rectifying some of these errors. In 2015, after the Academy of Motion Picture Arts and Sciences awarded all twenty acting nominations to white actors, the hashtag #OscarsSoWhite began to proliferate on the internet. Soon after, the Academy Awards became a veritable multicultural festival. *Moonlight*, featuring a largely Black cast, won Best Picture in 2016. The South Korean film *Parasite* got the nod in 2019. And in 2022 *Everything Everywhere All at Once*, with its mostly Asian cast, won the top prize. This dramatic change in what was for decades a highly conservative film industry bodes well for a future in which yellow-facing, black-facing, whitewashing, and other forms of cinematic cultural appropriation may be relegated to the dust bin of history.

VIEWPOINT 1

> "The Oscars matter, but the ceremony should not be conflated with the institution, where there is a discernible preference for creating white-centered media, and the practice of doing so is routinely defended as merely an economic calculation."

Whitewashing in Cinema Takes Many Forms
Lester Andrist

In this viewpoint, Lester Andrist expands on the usual definition of whitewashing to include four major ways in which Hollywood tends to showcase white stories and white actors. Andrist takes issue with the notions that the only color Hollywood producers see is green, and so they target their films to white audiences to maximize profit. Andrist sees this rationalization as shifting the blame for white dominance in cinema from producers and directors to the audience. Instead, he argues that "Hollywood films are directly implicated in shaping people's racialized preferences in the first place." Lester Andrist is director of the Master of Professional Studies in Public Safety Leadership and Administration program at the University of Maryland's department of sociology.

"What Is Whitewashing and Why Does It Matter?," by Lester Andrist, The Sociological Cinema, February 22, 2015. Reprinted by permission.

Cultural Appropriation

As you read, consider the following questions:

1. How does Andrist use the Oscars as a microcosm of Hollywood in general?
2. What are four types of whitewashing, according to Andrist?
3. Why does Andrist counsel his readers to step back and look at the big picture of all films produced by Hollywood?

In recent weeks, there has been an uptick in online discussions about whitewashing, due in no small part to the news that not a single person of color was nominated for an Academy Award this year. Soon after the nominations were announced, the hashtag #OscarsSoWhite began trending, where a number of people pointed out that this was in fact the second time in 20 years that the nominations list featured exclusively white actors. But pull back the Academy's plush red carpet a little further, and one finds it is the fifth time in 30 years this has happened. Pull it back even further and one finds that in the years between 1927 and 2012, 99 percent of women who have won "Best Actress" have been white, and the same is true for 91 percent of men who have won "Best Actor."

The charge being leveled against the Oscars is of racism; that consciously or not, members of the Academy consistently fail to appreciate and honor the work of non-white actors. The basis for the charge is that there have been enough nominations and enough awards given to detect a bias. That is, if Oscars were awarded like lottery winnings, by sheer chance alone non-white actors would take home a more proportionate share of the little statues, so there is cause to believe that somehow the creep of racial bias is contaminating the nomination process. The fact that 94 percent of voting members are white doesn't exactly ease fears that the Academy is playing racial favorites.

My aim here is not to contribute to the growing criticism of the Academy of Motion Picture Arts and Sciences. While the concerns of a whitewashed Oscars ceremony are certainly justified, in my view this criticism risks missing the forest for the trees. The more one obsesses about whether members of the Academy are racist or whether the ceremony is a racist production, the easier it is to miss the whitewashed media environment the Oscars celebrate. In other words, the Oscars matter, but the ceremony should not be conflated with the institution, where there is a discernible preference for creating white-centered media, and the practice of doing so is routinely defended as merely an economic calculation. There is some truth to the assertion that that Hollywood producers are simply giving people what they want. However, this explanation is far from complete, and I think there is cause for suspicion that the explanation shifts responsibility from the media makers to the media consumers.

In order to grab the problem at its root and expose it, it's necessary to define what is meant by whitewashing. In its simplest form, whitewashing refers to the tendency of media to be dominated by white characters, played by white actors, navigating their way through a story that will likely resonate most deeply with white audiences, based on their experiences and worldviews. There are four distinct types of whitewashing. My claim is that Hollywood is guilty of producing all of these types, and equally important is

Censoring Historical Examples of Racism in Film Doesn't Help Fight Racism or Cultural Appropriation

Scenes that show the late Mickey Rooney's caricature depiction of a Japanese character in "Breakfast at Tiffany's" were recently scrubbed from a version released by Channel 5 in the UK.

The free-to-air television network, which currently airs Audrey Hepburn's classic film via its streaming service My5, earned criticism after it decided to remove the scenes featuring the character of Mr. Yunioshi, Express reported.

continued on next spread

The 1961 American romantic comedy is regarded as an "iconic classic" by film critics and listed in the U.S. National Film Registry for being "culturally, historically or aesthetically" important. However, many have singled out Rooney's blatantly racist portrayal of Mr. Yunioshi in the film as its biggest flaw.

In one of the most notorious yellowface depictions on film, Rooney, a white man, had his eyes taped, wore buck teeth and used an exaggerated accent to deliver his lines.

The insulting representation has since been a part of conversations surrounding racist portrayals of Asian characters in mainstream entertainment, as previously explored by NextShark.

The portrayal was even dubbed "the godfather of the 'Ching-Chong' stereotype" by Jeff Yang in a 2014 Wall Street Journal piece.

However, some have pushed back against Channel 5's removal of the racist scenes, noting that it sets a dangerous precedent for similar censorship in the future.

Among those who criticized the move was filmmaker Terry Gilliam, former star of "Monty Python."

"Censorship seems to be a growth industry in Britain these days," he was quoted as saying. "To remove scenes of characters from films that had already survived the critical eye of past official censors seems absurd and dangerous. Who are the new censors? Who has given them the right to bowdlerize?"

According to Hepburn's son Sean Hepburn Ferrer, the film must be viewed from the perspective of people at the time it was filmed.

"That is the big problem today," he said. "Everything is looked at within the scope of one lifetime as if we were the most important point in the story. The film is what it is and you should put a warning at the beginning saying it was made in 1961 and these were the decisions made at the time."

Broadcasters have generally included a content warning at the beginning of the film but no one has done a full re-edit of it before.

[...]

"Network's decision to edit out yellow face character from 'Breakfast at Tiffany's' draws criticism," by Balraj Sohal, NextShark, November 26, 2021.

the fact that Hollywood also creates the conditions by which their continued production becomes almost inevitable.

First, whitewashing happens in films based on historical events, where white actors play the role of non-white characters. An exemplar of this first type is the classic movie, *Birth of a Nation*, where a number of white actors notoriously appeared in blackface. A more recent example is the film *Argo*, which recounts the CIA plot to rescue six Americans during the Iranian hostage crisis in 1981. In the film, Ben Affleck, a white man, plays the role of Tony Mendez, a Latino CIA officer who headed the operation. In addition to the incongruence between the real man and the actor, Tony Mendez's last name appears to be downplayed in the film.

A variation on this first type of whitewashing occurs in adaptations of written works of fiction. This happens when a fictional character from a novel is originally drawn or described as a person of color, yet in the live action adaptation, the character becomes inexplicably white. Sometimes the white actor pretends to be of a different race, as when Johnny Depp pretended to be a Native American man in *The Lone Ranger*. Other times the character's original racial identity is entirely abandoned and the character simply becomes white, as appears to be the case with *The Last Airbender*.

A second type of whitewashing can be observed in films that claim to be based on true stories. Here, the constellation of events that comprise a historical moment are reconfigured, forcing the audience to experience the story from a white perspective, as such, this type of whitewashing is a principal agent in shifting the public memory of real events. For example, *Dances with Wolves* ostensibly depicts a period of what has been euphemistically described by some historians as the Western Expansion, but is more accurately characterized as a patchwork of genocidal practices and policies by the United States government against the Native Peoples of North America. By inveigling its audience to experience this historical period through the eyes of a white protagonist, *Dances with Wolves* privileges the white experience. *Dances*, and other films like it, are whitewashed insofar as they succeed in prioritizing the white experience of witnessing this tragedy over the experiences of Native families who lived through it and died from it.

A third type of whitewashing can occur, even when the majority of characters in a film are played by black and brown actors. Here, the term refers to the observation that white actors secure all the major roles of a film, or they play the most well-rounded, complex characters of a film. Again, *Dances of Wolves* is an example of this type of film, but other examples include *The Last Samurai* and *Dangerous Minds*.

Finally, it is also possible to speak of whitewashing as a description of a genre or a particular film industry. Any given film might be dominated by white characters because some stories just happen to be told about white people. Similarly, it sometimes happens that white characters are protagonists in stories, and white actors are sometimes just the best actors for major roles. However, these films might justifiably be called whitewashed if the majority of films produced over a given span of time fit this pattern. In other words, whitewashing cannot always be discerned on a film-by-film basis. It is only after stepping back and looking at the films produced over the span of a period of time that one is able to see that a disproportionate number of films are being written from a white perspective, mostly feature white characters, or that speaking roles are disproportionately awarded to white actors.

There is an old cliche that the only color Hollywood executives see is green. Indeed, as I alluded to above, one common defense offered by those who make films is that they are simply giving the public what it wants. What is rarely discussed is that people are not simply born with fully formed preferences. The defense fails because Hollywood films are directly implicated in shaping people's racialized preferences in the first place. If it is true that the paying public truly wants white actors to dominate the silver screen, then Hollywood producers need to own up to the fact that they have played a central role in shaping that desire.

VIEWPOINT

> "At last, global Black culture was imagined by Hollywood as empowered and proud, and immune to the lasting effects of colonialism and forced migration."

Black Panther Was a Watershed Moment in Cinema—*Wakanda Forever* May Be Another

César Albarrán-Torres and Liam Burke

César Albarrán-Torres and Liam Burke write about the sequel to Black Panther, Wakanda Forever, *and suggest that the latter film may do for representations of early Mexican culture what* Black Panther *did for Africa. Instead of presenting facile clichés,* Black Panther *suggested the diversity and sophistication of Africa and its people. In casting a Mexican actor, Tenoch Huerta, to play Talokan in* Wakanda Forever, *the leader of his undersea civilization, director Ryan Coogan has brought a Latinx actor to the forefront in the same way* Black Panther *used Black actors. Albarrán-Torres and Burke hope that the movie will highlight the sophistication of pre-Columbian Mexican culture and lead to more fully realized parts for Latinx actors going forward. César Albarrán-Torres is a senior lecturer in the department of media and communication at Swinburne University of Technology in Melbourne, Australia. Liam Burke is an associate professor and cinema and screen studies at Swinburne University of Technology.*

"Black Panther and Brown Power – how Wakanda Forever celebrates pre-Columbian culture," by César Albarrán-Torres and Liam Burke, The Conversation, November 3, 2022. https://theconversation.com/black-panther-and-brown-power-how-wakanda-forever-celebrates-pre-columbian-culture-193443. Licensed under CC BY-ND 4.0 International.

Cultural Appropriation

As you read, consider the following questions:

1. How did *Black Panther* pave the way for more non-white heroes in film?
2. According to the viewpoint, how is pre-Columbian Mexican culture traditionally depicted?
3. What types of roles did the Latinx Tenoch Huerta typically play in his films?

Wakanda is back in cinemas, promising to deliver high-voltage action and trigger new discussions about how Hollywood represents other races and cultures. On November 10 Marvel's *Black Panther* will receive its long-awaited sequel, *Wakanda Forever*.

The first film was considered a landmark in how Black culture is represented in mainstream movies, breaking box office records and earning a Best Picture Oscar nomination. Now there are hopes that *Wakanda Forever* will have a similar impact in its depiction of pre-Columbian culture.

Directed by Ryan Coogler, the first *Black Panther* became an exemplar of ethnic diversity in mainstream cinema, as well as a watershed moment for how film interacts with everyday racial politics.

NBA icon and cultural commentator Kareem Abdul-Jabbar described *Black Panther* as a "cultural spearhead disguised as a thrilling action adventure."

> if you're white, you'll leave with an anti-'sh*thole' appreciation for Africa and African-American cultural origins. If you're black, you'll leave with a straighter walk, a gratitude for your African heritage and a superhero whom black children can relate to.

At last, global Black culture was imagined by Hollywood as empowered and proud, and immune to the lasting effects of colonialism and forced migration.

Reimagining Pre-Columbian Culture

After *Black Panther's* original star Chadwick Boseman tragically died in 2020, Marvel Studios had to reframe the future of the franchise, with Coogler deciding not to recast the lead role of T'Challa.

The story of *Wakanda Forever* centres around the political turmoil within the Afrofuturistic nation of Wakanda after the death of its king. Different factions must band together to repel the advances of a new enemy, the hidden undersea civilisation of Talokan, led by Namor (played by Mexican actor Tenoch Huerta).

In ancient Aztec culture, Talokan was the home of Tlaloc and his consort Chalchiuhtlicue, deities associated with rain and fertility. Marvel Studios has borrowed from pre-Columbian mythology to create a visually lush underwater civilisation based, in turn, on the character of Namor created by Bill Everett for 1939's Marvel Comics #1.

The combination of an Aztec worldview and an old Marvel antihero could prompt concerns regarding cultural appropriation. However, given how Ryan Coogler and Marvel celebrated Afro culture in *Black Panther*, there is an expectation that this new Marvel movie will subvert stereotypes and expand wider understanding of the often misunderstood ancient cultures of what is now the Americas (known as the Kuna term Abya Yala by Indigenous activists and organisations).

How *Black Panther* Unleashed a Wave of Non-White Heroes

Coogler's first film proved that inclusivity can also be profitable in Hollywood. Since *Black Panther*, a wave of blockbusters have been released featuring non-white heroes and challenge Western-centric conventions of action-adventure cinema.

In the past year alone, films such as *Shang-Chi* (based on Chinese mythology), *Black Adam* (set in a fictional Middle Eastern country), and *The Woman King* (about a group of 19th century

African female warriors) have provided a corrective to the historical disservice that Hollywood has done to so-called minorities.

Examples of mainstream cinema depicting pre-Columbian civilisations have been rare, and tend to cater to the tourist gaze by oversimplifying the history and richness of the Mesoamerican region. Films such as Mel Gibson's *Apocalypto*, Steven Spielberg's *Indiana Jones and the Kingdom of the Crystal Skull*, or the more recent live-action version of *Dora the Explorer* reduce complex civilisations later vanquished by European colonial forces to a handful of cliches.

These depictions misconstrue the history of civilisations that were highly advanced in science and technology compared to their European counterparts. They also have a negative impact on how millions of Latin Americans and Latinx individuals are represented onscreen and perceived in everyday life.

Namor Reframed as an Aztec-Inspired Antihero

First appearing in comic books in 1939, Namor has traditionally been depicted as the sometimes-villainous king of Atlantis. *Wakanda Forever* repositions Namor's underwater home to the Pacific Ocean and draws on Aztec and other pre-Columbian culture to realise this new Marvel hero.

The new Namor wears an Aztec-inspired headdress and armour, as well as facial piercings, and his underwater kingdom features buildings resembling Mesoamerican pyramids.

Mexican actor Tenoch Huerta, who stars as Namor, is one of the main voices of a social media campaign, #PoderPrieto ("Brown Power"), which fights against the white washing of the Mexican screen industry.

Contrary to fellow male Mexican actors who have been given diverse opportunities, up until now, the darker skinned Huerta has been typecast as a criminal and faced discrimination in the Mexican screen industry. Mexican film and television generally favours European-looking talent and systematically under-represents Indigenous Mexicans.

The release of *Wakanda Forever* coincides with renewed efforts by the incumbent Mexican government and activists to revisit the Indigenous and colonial histories of the country, and address systematic racism on and off-screen. For example, the federal government has demanded Spain and the Vatican apologise to Indigenous Mexicans over human rights abuses during the conquest over 500 years ago.

Huerta has spoken about the importance of inclusivity and representation of non-white characters in superhero movies. When Huerta was first unveiled to be playing the iconic character at San Diego Comic-Con he explained to the thousands of fans in attendance "I wouldn't be here without inclusion", and then switching to Spanish said "Thank you to all the Latin Americans – you guys crossed the river, and you all left everything you love behind. Thanks to that, I'm here."

The first *Black Panther* film was a milestone in Black representation on-screen, now it is hoped *Wakanda Forever* will be both a mirror and a spotlight for millions of Latin Americans, as well as for the vast Latinx diaspora around the world.

VIEWPOINT 3

> *"As a cultural practice, having white people play, replace and stereotype characters of colour obscures and erases their history, agency and power."*

Hollywood Has a Long History of Whitewashing

Dolores Tierney

In this viewpoint Dolores Tierney looks at the history of whitewashing in films. Whitewashing has always been the norm in Hollywood, and its practice continues today. In an early American film, Birth of a Nation *(which documents the beginnings of the Ku Klux Klan), Black characters are played by white actors in blackface. Even today, films such as* Doctor Strange *employ a white actor (Tilda Swinton) to play a non-white character. Tierney celebrates actor Ed Skrein's decision not to accept an offer to play the role of an Asian character. She wonders if others are "brave enough" to follow his lead. Dolores Tierney is a senior lecturer in film studies at the University of Sussex in the United Kingdom. She received her Ph.D. from Tulane University in New Orleans, Louisiana.*

"From *Breakfast at Tiffany's* to *Hellboy*: the ongoing problem of Hollywood 'whitewashing,'" by Dolores Tierney, The Conversation, September 5, 2017. https://theconversation.com/from-breakfast-at-tiffanys-to-hellboy-the-ongoing-problem-of-hollywood-whitewashing-83331. Licensed under CC BY-ND 4.0 International.

Is Cultural Appropriation a Problem in the Film Industry?

As you read, consider the following questions:

1. Why does Tierney suggest that John Wayne hardly had to even act in portraying his characters?
2. How did famous actor Charlton Heston participate in the whitewashing of roles?
3. What has to change in Hollywood, according to Tierney, to end the practice of whitewashing?

Actor Ed Skrein's much applauded withdrawal from the role of Asian character, Major Ben Daimio, in the *Hellboy* reboot has again highlighted the pervasive practice of "whitewashing" in contemporary Hollywood. Whitewashing is not new. It was a common practice in classical Hollywood where some of its most egregious examples include John Wayne as Genghis Khan in *The Conqueror* and Mickey Rooney as Mr Yunioshi in *Breakfast at Tiffany's*.

Audiences know instinctively that whitewashing is bad – hence the criticisms of other whitewashing films and the resulting hashtag #StarringJohnCho that went viral in spring 2016. As a cultural practice, having white people play, replace and stereotype characters of colour obscures and erases their history, agency and power. Although it is fair to reject whitewashing as false and offensive on these ideological grounds, to do so without further scrutiny does not allow us to explore the reasons why it exists.

Whitewashing happens in a number of ways. It can be the whitening through casting of a character who was originally a person of colour in historical or source material, as with Daimio in the new *Hellboy* or Major (Scarlett Johansson) in *Ghost in the Shell*. But it can also be the casting of a white actor to play a character of colour and the use of makeup, acting and other features of mise-en-scene, editing and narrative to draw on racial attributes – a practice often referred to as Yellow, Brown or Blackface. One early use of the latter includes D W Griffith's *Birth of Nation* in 1915: a white supremacist text that celebrates the founding of the Ku

Klux Klan. All the major black characters are played by white actors in Blackface.

Whiteness as the 'Norm'

Whitewashing exists historically and contemporaneously in Hollywood because from its early and silent periods Hollywood has, as Daniel Bernardi points out in *Classic Hollywood, Classic Whiteness* "constructed whiteness as the 'norm.'" What's more, Hollywood acting styles have shown "whiteness" to be the norm over "otherness." Look no further than John Wayne's impassive acting style in almost every film he appears in. We also see the assumption of whiteness as the norm in the idea that a white actor can play any character by simply "being" themselves or – if they are cast as a character of colour – by putting on an accent, makeup and other ethnically defining attributes and performance styles.

The flip side of whitewashing is that an actor of colour can only ever be cast as a character of colour and must perform in a way that marks or over determines their "difference" to the "norm." Thus, in John Ford's *Three Godfathers*, Mexican actor Pedro Armendariz – who actually grew up in the US and spoke English without an accent – has to put on a stereotypical Mexican accent and act with exaggerated gestures to play a Mexican character.

In the post World War II Hollywood of "liberal" race dramas, whitewashing allowed whiteness to be the clear moral voice of films, even when the narrative focus was on non-white characters. For instance, the sense of visible whiteness that whitewashing permitted is important to the 1958 movie *Touch of Evil*. In it, Charlton Heston plays Miguel Vargas, a Mexican police chief fighting against corruption and organised crime on both sides of the US/Mexico border.

Heston is visually "Mexicanised": he has curly hair, a moustache and darker skin. But as the hero of the film, it is important that Heston's whiteness is maintained, at least in terms of his star profile. Interestingly, Heston went almost directly to the character of

Whitewashing and Colorblind Casting on Broadway

Colorblind casting has three parts to it. The first part is where all casting begins: writing the characters. Some casting directors will try to match written descriptions of characters. In both of these examples, writers are justified in writing race into their characters, if they feel it is relevant. In a perfect world, writers would specify characters' races only when it aids the story's plot. Examples include Lin-Manuel Miranda's "Hamilton" and Caryl Churchill's "Cloud Nine," both of which have race written into characters to intentionally subvert conventions. However, writers also tell stories that have nothing to do with race, and leave the characters' ethnicity ambiguous.

This leads us to the second part of the issue: the casting process. Casting directors may logically abide by the writer's preferred race for the character — if this has been left ambiguous, they proceed to make a judgment based on what an audience may want to see or what makes the most sense. More often than not, white actors are cast in typical English-speaking roles, which has now become so much of a norm that directors subconsciously fill in the blank the writer has left behind.

Casting, the third component, is a political act that involves artistic choices, an expression of creative agency. A character's race, ambiguous or not, is not the same as an actor's race, and it doesn't have to be. Our concern should not be picking the right race for the right character. The problem is having white actors play parts that don't require whiteness. The solution could be more diverse writing and casting, or an intentional race-swapping so that we balance the scales.

However, blindness toward characters' races has often gone awry — instances that come to mind are the New York Gilbert and Sullivan Players' recently cancelled production of The Mikado, Cameron Crowe's "Aloha" and the upcoming film "Ghost in the Shell" starring Scarlett Johansson as a Japanese character. Rather than taking advantage of the opportunity to cast diverse actors in diverse roles, these films are examples of whitewashing. "The Mikado," for example has characters that are clearly Japanese, yet casts white actors. There is no political reason behind this, with an already disproportionate representation of white faces in the media.

[...]

"Whitewashing and color-blind casting on Broadway," by Michele Mendez, New York University, April 9, 2019.

Vargas after playing Moses in *The Ten Commandments* – another whitewashing role.

In the contemporary era, the casting of white actors in non-white roles persists. For this, we need look no further than Tilda Swinton as a Tibetan mentor in *Doctor Strange*. This despite protests from minority advocacy groups demanding more accurate representation and more parts for actors of colour.

The problem of whitewashing is frequently linked to the lack of diversity and institutional racism of a Hollywood film industry that is disproportionately white and male and in which people of colour are underrepresented – not just in front of the camera but also at the executive level and in producer and director roles.

It has been suggested that the key to solving Hollywood's whitewashing issue is recognising the achievements of those actors and film personnel of colour who are making films. This has been encapsulated in the hashtag #OscarsSoWhite. There needs to be structural change and more effort needs to be made at getting more minorities into the industry. Audiences also need to start signalling to film executives that the casting of white stars in non-white roles is not acceptable. Ed Skrein's rejection of whitewashing is to be applauded. We will now see if other actors are brave enough to follow his lead.

VIEWPOINT 4

> "Mickey Mouse—according to some researchers of that period, Mickey Mouse is a minstrel figure. And so that's why you see this sort of convention around cartoon characters in white gloves because that's part of vaudeville."

Why Blackface Endures

Gene Demby and Rachel Martin

In this viewpoint, which is an interview between Rachel Martin and Gene Demby, Demby discusses the long and problematic history of blackface and how the practice has endured to this day. Growing out of attempts to delegitimize and mock Black people, blackface was popular in 19th-century minstrel shows and came to Hollywood with Al Jolson and even, early on, Mickey Mouse. Though it is now seen as reprehensible and taboo, some white people have continued the practice. Such people may consider blackface good clean fun, but as Demby suggests, it is hurtful and demeaning to people of color. Gene Demby is a founding member of NPR's "Code Switch" team, where he serves as a host of the show's podcast. Rachel Martin is host of NPR's "Morning Edition" podcast.

©2019 National Public Radio, Inc. NPR news report titled "Why Blackface Endures" by Gene Demby and Rachel Martin was originally published on npr.org on February 8, 2019, and is used with the permission of NPR. Any unauthorized duplication is strictly prohibited.

Cultural Appropriation

As you read, consider the following questions:

1. What films and entertainers contributed to the early popularity of blackface entertainment?
2. According to Demby, how has making blackface a taboo contributed to its persistence among some white people?
3. How does the fact the many white people have only white friends contribute to the enduring nature of blackface?

Blackface has been a constant in American culture going all the way back to the country's founding. It's one of those inconvenient facts of U.S. history: a white supremacist cultural building block.

RACHEL MARTIN, HOST: Virginia's legislative black caucus wants answers about the numerous scandals embroiling that state's leaders. They want an investigation of the sex assault allegation against Lieutenant Governor Justin Fairfax. The caucus also called for more action from Attorney General Mark Herring following his apology for wearing blackface when he was 19. And they reiterated a call for Governor Ralph Northam to resign over his blackface controversy. Herring and Northam have said they were unaware of the harm they were doing at the time. I asked Gene Demby of NPR's Code Switch team about the history of blackface in America and why it has endured.

GENE DEMBY, BYLINE: It is a very long, complicated history. Blackface predates the Civil War, but it really gained traction as part of the minstrel shows that became wildly popular in the latter part of the 19th century. At one point, it was the most popular form of entertainment in the United States. Usually white performers, but not always, would apply some cork or some dye to their skins to blacken their skin. Maybe they'd apply some bright-red lipstick or wear white gloves to perform as these grotesques of what they imagined these newly emancipated black people to be. And it was meant to dehumanize. Blackface corresponds with the rise of Jim Crow segregation and with spectacle lynchings. And the popularity of blackface, like, continued well into the 20th century. By the 1920s, the vaudeville legend Al Jolson was the country's most popular entertainer.

MARTIN: Right.

DEMBY: Most of his act was in blackface. He was the star of the first talky, which he performed in blackface. And the conventions of vaudeville are so steeped in blackface imagery that you get Mickey Mouse in white gloves. Like, Mickey Mouse is...

MARTIN: Mickey Mouse.

DEMBY: Mickey Mouse (laughter).

MARTIN: Mickey Mouse is an outgrowth of blackface?

DEMBY: Mickey Mouse - according to some researchers of that period, Mickey Mouse is a minstrel figure. And so that's why you see this sort of convention around cartoon characters in white gloves because that's part of vaudeville. And so much of the DNA of vaudeville is blackface.

MARTIN: OK, so this is offensive. I mean, when African-Americans - when anyone who understands the history sees this, you understand that this is offensive. And yet, it happens. And yet, white people are still putting blackface on, I mean, in these recent examples. This was happening as recently as the '80s.

DEMBY: Right. I mean, one of the things we talk about a lot on the Code Switch podcast is the way that the civil rights movement created these taboos around open racism. So in the post-civil rights world, blackface moves away from public spaces and sort

Cultural Appropriation

of retreats to all-white spaces - spaces where there's not going to be a lot of social sanction for it. So...

MARTIN: Where no one raises an eyebrow. They're just...

DEMBY: Where there's just not going to be any black people around, right?

MARTIN: Right.

DEMBY: And just to back up a bit, that's a lot of spaces that white people inhabit. So a study by the Public Religion Research Institute in 2012 found that white people were significantly less likely to have friends of another race than were black or Latino people. In fact, three quarters of white people, the study found, had entirely white social networks. So the median white person's contact with black people is almost one of abstraction. And so these are spaces that are not really hard to cultivate - these super white spaces. And so when we're looking at these stories in the news, we're seeing fraternities at some college parties. These are spaces that are not necessarily codified as white spaces or resistant to people of color, but they're spaces that are functionally so.

MARTIN: Right. So that means in these all-white spaces, people - they're basically not held accountable. There's no one there to raise their hand and say, hi, that is super offensive to me.

DEMBY: Right. That's what seems to be happening. And of course there is this continuum, right? Some people are just oblivious. And some people are much more malicious, right? Obviously, we live in a time when someone posts something to social media, there's the slippage between these all-white contexts. And this larger social media space, on Twitter in particular, is much browner and younger than the country at large. And so these very different histories with these imageries are sort of butting up against each other.

MARTIN: So social media makes it easier to hold people accountable for racist behavior.

DEMBY: Yes. It also makes it easier for these images to spread in the world, right? I mean, the picture that seems to have ensnared Ralph Northam was buried in a medical school yearbook. Of course, now someone posts a racist picture to Snapchat or Twitter or Instagram, that can slip out of the sort of safe space into a much more contentious space very quickly. One of the things that is also happening here is that blackface has always had - especially in the post-civil rights world in which it was dangerous, right? That danger is part of the reason why people did it, right? It's part of the reason that people did it in these safe spaces.

MARTIN: Oh, so they knew there was something wrong about it.

DEMBY: Right. It's part of the sort of like - the thrill, I imagine.

MARTIN: The taboo.

DEMBY: The taboo of it, right? And so this is something that's true about the history of blackface minstrelsy - is that it was this element of mischief. This element of, like, we're doing something naughty is obviously much more insidious than that, but we're doing something naughty that always animated it, right? And so it's probably important for us to think about the ways in which racism can be animated by things that are fun, by things that...

MARTIN: Right, Mickey Mouse.

DEMBY: Mickey Mouse, right (laughter)?

MARTIN: Like, he's playful, and it's entertainment. And people are singing and dancing.

Cultural Appropriation

DEMBY: Absolutely. It becomes habituated in that way because it doesn't seem like malice. It doesn't seem like cruelty, right? And so you have something like, you know, the mascot of a sports team. Like, people do the tomahawk chop, and people do these other things that a lot of people from native communities will say are really offensive. And the defense for that is often that, like, this is fun for us; this is a thing that brings people together. But minstrel...

MARTIN: Right, we don't mean anything by it; it's not - yeah.

DEMBY: That's right. It's just in good fun. But that's always been important to the way that people have justified these very mocking racist images.

MARTIN: Gene Demby from NPR's Code Switch team. Thanks so much, Gene.

DEMBY: Thank you, Rachel.

VIEWPOINT 5

> "In Hollywood, cultural appropriation was common and strictly a one-way street: always white performers darkening their skin to play characters of color, even when those characters were historical figures — Genghis Khan, say, portrayed in The Conqueror (1956) by John Wayne with a gunslinger's swagger and a Midwestern drawl."

In Defense of Cross-Cultural Casting
Bob Mondello

In this viewpoint, Bob Mondello speaks out in favor of cross-cultural casting. This type of casting has always occurred on stage and in film, except that in the past, it was always white actors who were cross-culturally cast, playing the roles of Black people, Asian people, and more. The only difference between this and today's cross-cultural and colorblind casting, Mondello writes, is that now it is BIPOC actors who may be cast in white roles, a striking development that has turned the entertainment world upside down. But when the Broadway play Hamilton *cast BIPOC actors in white roles, the public ate it up, suggesting that we are ready for such innovative entertainment. If handled well, and in the hands of skillful actors, cross-cultural casting does not interfere with the storytelling and*

©2021 National Public Radio, Inc. NPR news report titled "The Only 'New' Thing About Cross-Cultural Casting Is Who's Getting the Roles" by Bob Mondello was originally published on npr.org on July 15, 2021, and is used with the permission of NPR. Any unauthorized duplication is strictly prohibited.

Cultural Appropriation

offers opportunity for all. Bob Mondello reviews movies and covers the arts for NPR.

As you read, consider the following questions:

1. How has there always been cross-cultural casting in theater and film?
2. What is color-conscious casting?
3. What are some examples of color-conscious casting in contemporary cinema?

From the debates and the hype on social media about unconventional casting choices lately, you might think the world was about to spin off its axis.

If *Slumdog Millionaire* star Dev Patel takes a seat at the Round Table in *The Green Knight*, does that mean King Arthur recruited knights of Indian descent in the 12th century?

And is Mindy Kaling really voicing the brainiac title character in a Scooby-Doo spinoff called *Velma*? And producing it too?

And didn't casting Jamaican British actress Jodie Turner-Smith as the doomed wife of King Henry VIII in the British miniseries *Anne Boleyn* violate some unspoken rule about historical realism?

"For what it's worth," wrote *The Guardian*'s Lucy Mangan in a review of that last opus, "I am aware that Anne Boleyn wasn't black, but I'm also aware that she wasn't Claire Foy, Merle Oberon, Helena Bonham Carter or any of the other women who have played her over the years, and my brain is not unduly upset by any of it."

What Mangan could have added is that social media dithering over these announcements is at best misguided, since cross-cultural casting is about as old as casting itself.

Audiences Have a Long History of Suspending Disbelief

In the fifth century B.C., when the Greek playwright Aeschylus needed a top-notch defense attorney for his leading tragedian in the trilogy *The Oresteia*, he settled on the god Apollo.

Not to put too fine a point on it, but this is not a choice a playwright would make if he were worried about verisimilitude in casting. And why would he be? Live theater has always assumed the audience can make imaginative leaps, whether it's depicting a deus ex machina, a warrior king who rants or Founding Fathers who rap.

Hamilton, of course, is a special case: a Broadway musical famous not just for putting hip-hop in the mouths of Thomas Jefferson and George Washington, but for matching Black and brown faces to those historic white characters.

For composer-lyricist Lin-Manuel Miranda, that casting decision was baked into the show's content from the moment he decided that the characters would rap.

"Hip-hop was uniquely suited to telling Hamilton's immigrant narrative," he told Fresh Air's Terry Gross. "And it's incredibly meaningful to then populate our live show with Black and brown artists ... because hip-hop is a Black art form and, also, it's our country too."

"Every time I write a piece of theater, I'm trying to get us on the board."

Inclusion became *Hamilton*'s calling card, and diverse audiences soon made it a worldwide phenomenon, an outcome that seems natural in retrospect but that flew in the face of decades of theater practice.

Theatrical White Privilege at Play

In 1986, when the performers union Actors' Equity convened the first National Symposium on Non-Traditional Casting, it noted that more than 90% of actors who had been hired in the U.S. in the previous five years were white. And it presented scenes designed to help theater-*makers* consider other possibilities: in Tennessee Williams' *Cat on a Hot Tin Roof*, for instance, James Earl Jones as Southern patriarch Big Daddy, opposite white actor Stephen Collins as his son Brick.

New York magazine critic John Simon did not see this scene, having pointedly declined to attend the symposium, but he told NPR's Carole Zimmer at the time that the whole notion struck him as ridiculous.

"You cannot create the illusion of a Joan of Arc with a Black actress," he stated flatly. "It doesn't work, unless they can make themselves up to 'pass.' But this they can no longer do because their ethnic pride forbids it."

To be clear, Simon had no problem with Jeanne d'Arc, who was burned at the stake at age 19 in France, being played by an actress in her 30s, in English. For him, skin color was the one deal-breaker.

His attitude regrettably held sway for years despite the efforts of the symposium's attendees to make dents in the armor of white theatrical privilege. It would be decades before Jones finally got to play Big Daddy for a paying crowd. But then, actors of color were used to waiting, even for roles for which they were ideally suited.

Choosing Blackface over Black Actors

Take Othello, arguably the most famous Black character in theatrical history. Shakespeare penned his tragedy in 1603, and it's rife with references — "an old black ram / Is tupping your white ewe" — to the title character's African origins.

Would it surprise you to know that it took more than two centuries before the part was played in England by a Black actor? New Yorker Ira Aldridge was the first, having relocated to London because in the early 1800s, Black actors couldn't get work on American stages.

The reaction? British critics had a problem with Aldridge's Othello because of his race(!) — in the absence of Black English actors, they'd grown accustomed to the Moor being played as a light-skinned Arab.

Times would change, casting choices too, but slowly. When the great African American actor Paul Robeson played Othello in the 1930s, he was the exception, not the rule. And things moved slower still on-screen.

Orson Welles was one of many white actors to play the Moor in blackface on film and television more than a century after Aldridge. Laurence Olivier was nominated for an Oscar for playing him in blackface in 1965. Anthony Hopkins played him on television in 1981 to general acclaim.

Big Screen, but Limited Imagination

In Hollywood, cultural appropriation was common and strictly a one-way street: always white performers darkening their skin to play characters of color, even when those characters were historical figures — Genghis Khan, say, portrayed in *The Conqueror* (1956) by John Wayne with a gunslinger's swagger and a Midwestern drawl.

Surely there was an Asian actor who was a better fit for that Mongol warrior, but never mind — Burt Lancaster had just played the title character in *Apache*, and no one had batted an eye.

Even after that sort of grotesquerie became untenable, exceptions were made for white actors in the classics. And if the film industry saw fit to hand Othello, the theater's most famous Black leading role, to the likes of Olivier and Hopkins, what hope could actors of color have for roles not specifically conceived for them — say, a Black James Bond?

That's a question Idris Elba has been fielding for so long that he has more or less aged out of contention. And sure, he has the detective miniseries *Luther,* as well as a place in both the Marvel Cinematic Universe and the DC Extended Universe, to console him. But as big a star as Elba is, was anyone auditioning him when he was in his 30s to play Mr. Darcy? There's a whole world of literary parts he's unlikely ever to be considered for.

New Possibilities in a New Generation

It's something you might also have said until recently about *Slumdog Millionaire* star Dev Patel. Imagine him being cast in Dickens? Preposterous, until it happened. Director Armando Iannucci decided on colorblind casting for *The Personal History of David Copperfield*, filling the screen behind Patel's dashing Dickensian hero with Black aristocratic mothers of white sons, Asian fathers of Black daughters — giving the film's world far more diversity than even mid-empire London would have possessed. It interferes with the storytelling not at all, and, says Iannucci, it offers opportunity evenhandedly.

"There is such a lot of talent there," he told an interviewer shortly after the film's premiere at the Toronto International Film Festival. "And Dev himself said, normally in a film like this he'd be carrying a tea tray, standing at the back. And for a man of his talent and ability, that's just tragic to think that that's a possibility."

Color-*blind* casting of the sort that Iannucci is practicing is one way to counter that.

Another is color-*conscious* casting, where roles are assigned nontraditionally to make a point. That's what producer Shonda Rhimes did in the Emmy-nominated *Bridgerton*, desegregating costume drama by using the real Black ancestry of Britain's Queen Charlotte (wife to King George III, who just a few years before the ones depicted in the series had been dealing with those pesky American revolutionaries depicted in *Hamilton*) to imagine a Black British aristocracy in waistcoats and petticoats.

"We were two separate societies divided by color," says Adjoa Andoh's Lady Danbury, "until the king fell in love with one of us."

She sees this as evidence that love conquers all. Her nephew, Simon, who has been dallying with the show's white leading lady, is skeptical.

"The king may have elevated us from novelties in their eyes to, now, dukes and royalty. And at that same whim, he may just as easily change his mind."

And there's always the risk that something similar could happen with nontraditional casting. Which is why the last few months have been so bracing — *Bridgerton, Copperfield, Anne Boleyn*. Later this month, Dev Patel's Sir Gawain will quaff ale with King Arthur in David Lowery's *The Green Knight*. As the weather cools, Elba, Regina King and Delroy Lindo will head a star-studded Black cast in *The Harder They Fall*, an attempt to reclaim the Western.

And before year's end, Denzel Washington will star opposite Frances McDormand in a presumed awards-contender: Shakespeare's *The Tragedy of Macbeth*, directed by McDormand's husband, Joel Coen.

Macbeth is a role that Ira Aldridge — that first Black Othello in the 1800s — had to wear white makeup to play. So there has been progress, though it has certainly been long in coming — more opportunity always on the way, but just out of reach.

"Tomorrow," as Washington will soon intone. "And tomorrow, and tomorrow ..."

Cultural Appropriation

Periodical and Internet Sources Bibliography

The following articles have been selected to supplement the diverse views presented in this chapter.

Marc Bernardin, "Wes Anderson's 'Isle of Dogs': Is Cultural Appropriation Hollywood's Next Big Battleground?," *Hollywood Reporter*, March 29, 2018. https://www.hollywoodreporter.com/movies/movie-news/isle-dogs-is-cultural-appropriation-hollywoods-next-big-battleground-1098228/.

Rayna Breuer, "How Disney Represents Other Cultures," *DW*, December 9, 2021. https://www.dw.com/en/how-disney-represents-other-cultures/a-60065256.

Emi P. Cummings, "Color-Blind Casting Isn't 'Woke' — It's Racist," *Harvard Crimson*, December 9, 2020. https://www.thecrimson.com/article/2020/12/9/unpop-opinion-color-blind-casting/.

Bill DeYoung, "'Mr. Yunioshi' Explores Hollywood's Asian Stereotypes," *Catalyst*, September 12, 2022. https://stpetecatalyst.com/mr-yunioshi-explores-hollywoods-asian-sterotypes/.

Claire Gillespie, "What Is Whitewashing, and Why Is It Harmful? Here's What Experts Say," *Prestige*, June 7, 2021. https://www.prestigeonline.com/hk/people/what-is-whitewashing-and-why-is-it-harmful/.

Joseph Learoyd, "From *Aladdin* to *Moana*: Cultural Representation in Disney Animations," *Headstuff*, January 11, 2023. https://headstuff.org/entertainment/film/from-aladdin-to-moana-cultural-representation-in-disney-animations/.

Emma H. Lu, "Does 'Avatar' Use Blueface? Cultural Appropriation and White Saviorism in Film," *Harvard Crimson*, February 2, 2021. https://www.thecrimson.com/article/2023/2/21/avatar-the-way-of-water-blueface-cultural-appropriation/.

Kenan Malik, "In Defense of Cultural Appropriation," *New York Times*, June 14, 2017. https://www.nytimes.com/2017/06/14/opinion/in-defense-of-cultural-appropriation.html.

Sonia Rao, "'The Simpsons' and 'Big Mouth' Are Recasting Nonwhite Roles. But It's About More than Finding the Right Voices," *Washington Post*, July 2, 2020. https://www.washingtonpost.com/

arts-entertainment/2020/07/02/the-simpsons-jenny-slate-voice-actors-recast/.

Steve Rose, "'The Idea that It's Good Business Is a Myth' – Why Hollywood Whitewashing Has Become Toxic," *Guardian*, August 29, 2017. https://www.theguardian.com/film/2017/aug/29/the-idea-that-its-good-business-is-a-myth-why-hollywood-whitewashing-has-become-toxic.

Adam Starkey, "'Ferrari' Producer Defends Casting of Adam Driver Against 'Cultural Appropriation' Criticism," *NME*, September 5, 2023. https://www.nme.com/news/film/ferrari-producer-defends-casting-adam-driver-over-italian-actors-3493410.

Tom Taylor, "Breakfast at Tiffany's: A Sign of the Times or Racist, Imperialist Propaganda?," *Farout Magazine*, October 5, 2022. https://faroutmagazine.co.uk/breakfast-at-tiffanys-racist-imperialist-propaganda/.

Zach Vasquez, "Latinxploitation: On the Complicated History of Whitewashing and Brownface in the Movies," *Crooked Marquee*, August 10, 2020. https://crookedmarquee.com/latinxploitation-on-the-complicated-history-of-whitewashing-and-brownface-in-the-movies/.

Suzy Woltmann, "What Are Colorblind and Color-Conscious Casting?," *Backstage*, December 1, 2023. https://www.backstage.com/magazine/article/color-blind-casting-76238/.

CHAPTER 4

Are Team Names and Mascots that Use Cultural Appropriation Acceptable?

Chapter Preface

While McGill University is perhaps not well-known in the United States except in academic circles, it has quite a reputation in the country to the north. In fact, McGill is quite commonly referred to as the Harvard of Canada. The school has numerous sports teams that supplement its educational curricula, and if you go to their website, you will see the team nickname prominently displayed: the Redbirds. Their mascot is the Martlet, a mythological bird without feet that never lands but continuously flies about.

But this moniker and its attendant mascot were not always associated with McGill. In fact, just a decade ago the team name was this: Redmen. Interestingly, the name was not originally offensive at all. It was chosen because the prestigious university was named for James McGill, a redheaded Scotsman. But in the 1940s, this all changed. According to McGill professor Suzanne Morton: "There's a new football coach hired from the United States, and he wants to make football more spectacle. He wants crowds. And so we have the input of really explicit Indigenous images onto, particularly, the football team."

From this point forward, Indigenous imagery became associated with McGill sports teams. The men's teams were called "Indians." The women's team became "Super Squaws."

"You have images of fierceness, bravery, savagery," Morton continued, "The marching band, all of a sudden, has a cartoon of an Indigenous man in a McGill uniform — braids flying, carrying a football. You get new songs which talk horribly about things like scalping and warpath."

In 1991, a campaign to rid McGill teams of their offensive iconography succeeded in having the Redmen logo removed. "The billboard-sized Indian head in the gym went away. The football and hockey helmets were changed to sport the McGill crest. But the Redmen name stayed," according to former student Matthew

Stock. Indigenous students who matriculated at McGill—and even joined their sports teams—were confronted by this ubiquitous, offensive nickname for their teams. In the last decade, the efforts to permanently delete "Redmen" from McGill University grew. A task force recommended replacing the name in 2017; there was a student demonstration in 2018. Then, finally, after fits and starts, the Redmen name was retired in 2019.

Not all Indigenous team names are equally offensive. Contrast this situation with that of Central Michigan University (CMU), located in Mount Pleasant, Michigan, a small city of 21,000 about an hour north of Lansing and two and a half hours northwest of Detroit. CMU's team nickname is proudly, unabashedly, the Chippewas, after a Native American tribe that is indigenous to the region. In the 20th century, the name drew much criticism. But as of 2024, there are no plans to replace the team name. Why the difference?

When controversy first arose in the 1970s and 1980s, the Michigan Civil Rights Commission recommended replacing the name. Instead, the university decided to fully embrace the Chippewa name, enacting educational programs in conjunction with the Saginaw Chippewa Tribal Council. Orientation programs were also created to educate CMU students and staff about Chippewa culture, and CMU's Native American logos and pep-band music that reflected stereotypes were dropped as well.

Saginaw Chippewa Indian Tribe chief Timothy Davis has given his blessing to CMU's use of his tribe's moniker: "The partnership goes back many decades, and I see the value in the education and outreach opportunities in sharing of the nickname." According to CMU president Bob Davies, "The tribe is the one that makes the decision of how we use the identifier. We do not have a mascot. We handle the name with a great deal of respect."

And so we have a tale of two colleges, one of which dropped an offensive name, and the other which promoted a partnership with Native Americans. Debating the topic on a Reddit message board, one "redditor" summarized the situation neatly: "Actual tribal names: not offensive. Racial slurs: offensive. It's not complicated."

But this summary may be an optimistic oversimplification. Awareness of cultural appropriation has grown so rapidly and people can be so quick to take offense that perhaps the time will come when there will be no Central Michigan University Chippewas, or University of Utah Utes, or Florida State Seminoles.

VIEWPOINT 1

> "Teams often claim that they are in fact honouring American Indian heritage and traditions, but this argument has come close to collapse under the weight of ongoing activism and academic research into the harmful effects of racial stereotyping and caricaturing."

Native American Mascots and Team Names Are Common in North America and Europe, but That Is Finally Changing

Sam Hitchmough

In this viewpoint, Sam Hitchmough explains how Washington's NFL team changed its name from the Washington Redskins to the Washington Commanders, signaling a change in what people think of Native American-related mascots and team names. He asserts that the campaigns against the use of Indigenous imagery have had a ripple effect. The use of American Indian imagery and names has a long history in sports in North America and across the Atlantic in Europe. The campaigns against using these names and images began in the 1960s and 1970s, but has gained power in recent years. Hitchmough argues that the fact that teams in the UK and other European countries use the same names and imagery drives home

"Sports teams are finally scrapping Native American mascots – on both sides of the Atlantic," by Sam Hitchmough, The Conversation, February 7, 2022, https://theconversation.com/sports-teams-are-finally-scrapping-native-american-mascots-on-both-sides-of-the-atlantic-176083. Licensed under CC BY-ND 4.0 International.

Are Team Names and Mascots that Use Cultural Appropriation Acceptable?

the fact that these are stereotypical depictions of Indigenous people stripped of context, which is a major part of the problem. Sam Hitchmough is an associate professor of modern U.S. history at the University of Bristol in the UK, where he researches and teaches Native American and African American history.

As you read, consider the following questions:

1. According to Hitchmough, what factors caused the Washington NFL team to change their name?
2. Why does Hitchmough say the use of Native American names and imagery for sports teams in the UK is incongruous?
3. What does Hitchmough mean when he says "mascots 'freeze' American Indians in the past"?

After two years of simply being called the Washington Football Team, the US capital's American football franchise has unveiled its new name and branding: the Washington Commanders. Following over 80 years known as the Washington Redskins, the offensive name was removed in 2020 as a result of sustained activism from American Indian groups, and eventually, the threat of corporations withdrawing sponsorship.

The rebrand is one of the most high-profile in a wave of professional sports teams abandoning their use of American Indian team names and imagery. Also in 2020, the Kansas City Chiefs withdrew their mascot, and in July 2021 the Cleveland baseball team changed its name from "Indians" to "Guardians". Some US states are now passing legislation banning public schools from using Native-related mascots.

The ripple effects of these activist campaigns reaching British shores have strengthened. On January 27, the Exeter Chiefs Premiership rugby union club announced that they will remove all American Indian logos and related imagery. The name Chiefs will remain, but will now instead be associated with regional history, representing the Celtic Iron Age Dumnonii Tribe.

Indeed, the use of names and mascots associated with indigenous communities around the world is extensive. The pattern of use in Europe – including the Bürstadt Redskins in Germany and KAA Gent football) in Belgium – is one where instead of indigenous groups self-representing, the images are adopted by teams with no connection to these groups. This has been linked with ideas of ongoing colonialism and conceptual control.

Campaigns against the use of American Indian imagery are rooted in the Red Power era of the 1960s-70s. Efforts have focused not only on team names and logos, but also the paraphernalia and activities that fans are encouraged to buy into. The Atlanta Braves' controversial, but still widespread, "tomahawk chop" is just one example.

The use of this imagery in the UK appears incongruous given the degree of historic, cultural and geographic separation from the indigenous population of America. There is no link between the Exeter team and Native America, but the branding ran from the team mascot to crystal brandy glasses, golfing gloves and baby's

Is Removing an Offensive Mascot Enough?

AILSA CHANG, HOST: Now that Cleveland's baseball team revealed its new name, some of the spotlight has turned to Kansas City football. As KCUR's Luke Martin reports, this week, the Chiefs retired a well-known fixture at Arrowhead Stadium.

LUKE MARTIN, BYLINE: The retirement is that of a horse named Warpaint. She's been doing victory runs after Chiefs touchdowns since 2009. But at a press conference Monday, team president Mark Donovan says those days are over. The move is part of a years-long evolution in the team's use of much criticized Native American imagery. But Donovan stresses that the evolution does not include changing the team's name.

Are Team Names and Mascots that Use Cultural Appropriation Acceptable?

MARK DONOVAN: We'll continue to take the path we've taken educating ourselves, educating our fans, creating opportunities to create awareness.

MARTIN: For eight years, the team has consulted the American Indian Community Working Group, and slowly, some change has come. Last year, the team banned headdresses and Native-inspired face paint in the stadium. But the notorious tomahawk chop chant is still criticized by many. That progress is too slow for Gaylene Crouser, executive director of the Kansas City Indian Center.

GAYLENE CROUSER: They're just kind of, I think, trying to placate the community at this point. How much racism are we going to tolerate?

MARTIN: This isn't the first time a horse has been retired. There was no Warpaint in the late '90s and early 2000s. The National Congress of American Indians and plenty of others, including Crouser, want the Chiefs to change their name and cut out Native imagery altogether.

CROUSER: And it can't be that hard to find something that's not a stereotype of a human being.

MARTIN: As for the fans, well, they appear to be split. Joe Beckerman has been going to home games for years. Warpaint's retirement wasn't a surprise to him.

JOE BECKERMAN: Yeah, the horse could go. That was getting old anyway.

MARTIN: But Beckerman doesn't think the Chiefs need a name change, and he's not worried about adjusting to a post-Warpaint era. For at least some of those fans, Warpaint's retirement is a step in the right direction, moving away from imagery many find offensive. For NPR News, I'm Luke Martin in Kansas City.

"Kansas City Chiefs Removed Their Offensive Mascot, But Have No Plans to Change Name," by Annabel Rackham, National Public Radio Inc. (NPR), January 21, 2020.

bibs. A number of other British sports teams use American Indian imagery, such as the Tees Valley Mohawks basketball team and the Whitley Warriors ice hockey team.

Using such names and images in the UK, shorn of all historic context, ensures that the use of American Indian branding becomes more pointedly associated with the stereotypical attributes that the teams seek to exploit: bravery, savagery, ruggedness and the "warrior spirit". Teams often claim that they are in fact honouring American Indian heritage and traditions, but this argument has come close to collapse under the weight of ongoing activism and academic research into the harmful effects of racial stereotyping and caricaturing.

Changing Times

In 2016, the London-based Streatham Redskins hockey team rebranded to the RedHawks, as a result of the growing campaign against the Washington team. Exeter have now followed suit, but only after vocally resisting calls to change. In the same year Rachel Herrmann, an American academic working in the UK, published a critical blog post about the Exeter branding. The piece provoked a largely hostile response everywhere from local newspapers to national morning chat shows.

Herrmann's blog post echoed many of the arguments that campaign groups in the US had been making for years. Mascots "freeze" American Indians in the past, connect them to a pre-modern landscape, and conceptually deny them existence in the present: the very idea of American Indians is welded to the idea of the great plains and the frontier. Activists and academics also discuss the idea of "playing Indian", where white men and women perform their version of "Indianness" by putting "war paint" on their faces, wearing war bonnets and participating in the tomahawk chop. Many argue this act of "red-facing" is equivalent to blackface minstrelsy.

In June 2020, fans established the Exeter Chiefs for Change group. Working with many indigenous activists, they quickly gave added impetus to the campaign for change.

In July 2020, the Exeter club stated that their use of American Indian imagery was "highly respectful", but admitted that the mascot, Big Chief, should be removed. The National Congress of American Indians (NCAI), America's largest and oldest American Indian civil rights organisation, wrote directly to the club in autumn 2021 urging them to remove all branding. The NCAI had helped to decisively shift public opinion in the US on the issue with a prominent campaign video released in 2013.

In mid-October 2021, the Exeter club's chairman, Tony Rowe, wondered: "Are all these people really getting upset in North America? I don't quite believe that."

Ignorance around such critical issues owing to geographical distance is no longer an excuse. The change now occurring on both sides of the Atlantic is proof of this.

VIEWPOINT

> "The organization had what they called Chief Noc-A-Homa as a mascot from 1950 until 1986. Although many thought it was a playful mix of Native American names and baseball terminology, many found the mascot's name and costume offensive."

Ten Controversial Sports Team Names that Have Been or Should Be Changed

Justin Findlay

In this viewpoint, Justin Findlay lists ten team names that have proven highly controversial. (To be fair, several of these organizations, including the Washington football team, the Cleveland baseball team, and McGill University sports teams have changed their names since the viewpoint was originally published in 2017.) Many of these names, often taken from aboriginal peoples of America, Canada, or Mexico, have been offensive to the very people whom they are supposedly glorifying. Justin Findlay has a bachelor's degree in political science and media and communications, specializing in modern Middle Eastern politics. He writes for World Atlas.

"10 Of the Most Controversial Team Names in Sporting History," by Justin Findlay, WorldAtlas, October 30, 2017. Reprinted by permission.

Are Team Names and Mascots that Use Cultural Appropriation Acceptable?

As you read, consider the following questions:

1. Which of the names listed, according to the viewpoint, seems to be the least offensive? Why?
2. Besides the names themselves, what other features of team iconography have offended Indigenous people?
3. According to Findlay, how is the name "Eskimos" offensive?

Many of these sports teams were named at a time when institutional racism or tension was not recognized and given proper discourse within society. Many of the teams featured on this list feature stereotypical names involving race, and more specifically, the native aboriginal races. A lot of people argue that this type of institutionalized stereotyping of race leads to further marginalization within society. Take a look at some of the most controversial and offensive sports team names in history below.

10. Washington Redskins

The Washington Redskins is a team that plays in the National Football League (NFL) of the United States and has been using this name and logo since 1937. The controversy stems from the meaning of the word "redskin", a term that has been deemed to have an offensive meaning towards the Native American peoples, and as such many tribes and native organizations have condemned the use of the name and image for decades.

9. Cleveland Indians

This logo draws criticism because it is seen as a racial stereotype in a caricature. Chief Wahoo, the character featured in the logo, depicts a Native American with red skin and large white teeth. Many Native American groups within the United States have called for the team to change their logo and name for the past 40 years. When the Cleveland Indians made the World Series in 2016 for the first time in 19 years, the logo was on full display for the entire country, and many have now called for it to be changed.

8. Chicago Blackhawks

The Chicago Blackhawks of the National Hockey League (NHL) is perhaps the least offensive on this list. The Blackhawks are named after the 333rd Machine Gun Battalion that received the moniker of "Blackhawk Division," nicknamed after a Native America Chief of the same name. Chief Black Hawk was well-known for his bravery in the face of seemingly improbable odds.

7. Edmonton Eskimos

The Edmonton Eskimos are a professional gridiron team that plays in the Canadian Football League (CFL). The name of the team can be traced back over a century to 1903 and could have even been used as a team name as far back as 1892. The president of the National Inuit Organization of Canada (Inuit Tapiriit Kanatami) has claimed that the term is derogatory and that is also symbolizes colonialist policies of racism. The term Inuit is much preferred by people of this origin, with the term eskimo now considered to be somewhat offensive.

6. Seattle Thunderbirds

The Seattle Thunderbirds are a junior ice-hockey team that competes in the Western Hockey League (WHL). Their logo consists of a carving of a thunderbird, a legendary Native American creature, with various Native American imagery such as warpaint and feathers resembling that of a war bonnet imposed within the logo. The team is the reigning WHL champion and is known for their loyal and reasonably sized fan base. Their team name and logo have managed to stay relatively uncontroversial and under the radar as, as a junior hockey team, they are nowhere near the financial juggernaut of some other organizations within this article.

5. Bristol Aztecs

The Bristol Aztecs is a British based American football team that competes in the British American Football League (BAFL). The Aztecs were people who dominated large areas of Mexico from the

14th to 16th centuries. The logo for the team is one that conjures up images of indigenous cultures and practices although this team is based all the way over in England, which makes the name choice somewhat confusing. Fans of the team will also use imagery and costumes to portray an 'Aztec' while watching games. The Aztec people may be long gone, but this logo is still be seen as offensive due to the appropriation of indigenous imagery.

4. Kansas City Chiefs

The Kansas City Chiefs are an American football team that plays in the National Football League (NFL). Their early mascot was eventually replaced in 1989, however their name and logo remain. The logo consists of an arrowhead and tomahawk which are both cultural symbols of the Native American people. Many fans of the Chiefs will also dress up as Native American stereotypes to attend games. Some pundits have suggested that Kansas City should be the first team in the NFL to change their name and lead the way in terms of changing these types of names within professional sports.

3. Atlanta Braves

The Atlanta Braves baseball team plays in Major League Baseball's National (MLB) League and the team has been known as such since 1912. The original name was meant to signify a term for a Native American warrior. Their logo also uses culturally sensitive imagery such as a tomahawk which is seen as inappropriate due to the organization gaining profit from uniform and merchandise sales that carry the image. The organization had what they called Chief Noc-A-Homa as a mascot from 1950 until 1986. Although many thought it was a playful mix of Native American names and baseball terminology, many found the mascot's name and costume offensive.

2. McGill Redmen

The McGill Redmen is the name given to many different men's sports teams from the University of McGill in Montreal, Canada. Many from the university will claim that the original Redmen sports teams name came from the fact that the athletes wore red clothing, and that only 2 of the 48 sports teams using the Redman name in the history of the university have used logos that feature some sort of aboriginal imagery. However, the term is generally used as a racist name for the aboriginal people of Canada, and many people believe the name should be changed to something less offensive.

1. Florida State Seminoles

A Seminole is a member of a Native American tribe located in Florida and are also well known for their bravery and perseverance. For almost 70 years, Florida State University has named its sports teams after a Native American tribe, the Seminoles. Several representatives met with the university in the 1980s and 1990s and actually gave their blessing to use Seminole imagery for the university's sports teams. However, some of the Seminole disagree with the use of their cultural imagery.

VIEWPOINT 3

> "The mascots connected to these names are often racist caricatures. A large body of research has shown that Native-themed mascots perpetuate stereotypes and have negative effects on Native youth and how they view themselves and their communities."

Progress Is Being Made in Changing Offensive Team Names

Encyclopædia Britannica

This viewpoint is about how, despite staunch resistance from many team owners, Native American activists have made substantial gains in ridding sports of offensive names and mascots. Professional sports teams are the most popular and glaring examples, but activists have also had an effect on changing college team names and high school names as well. The NCAA has enforced rules on removing offensive names, as have numerous states. Still, as of 2023, almost two thousand schools, mostly secondary, still use Native American nomenclature and mascots. Encyclopædia Britannica *is the world's oldest continuously published encyclopedia. The company also owns the American dictionary publisher Merriam-Webster, and though historically British, it is now based in Chicago, Illinois.*

"Native American mascot controversy," Encyclopædia Britannica. Reprinted by permission.

Cultural Appropriation

As you read, consider the following questions:

1. What are some of the ways activists pressured teams to drop offensive team names?
2. What colleges led the way in removing offensive names and mascots?
3. What laws have states passed in an effort to get secondary schools to change their team names?

Native American mascot controversy is conflict arising from the use of Native American-themed logos, mascots, and names by sports teams. Native-themed team names and mascots have been widely used throughout sports, from elementary schools to professional franchises. These names may refer to tribal nations (such as Sioux or Huron) or categories of people (braves, warriors, or chiefs). The most common names are the general terms Indians or warriors.

The mascots connected to these names are often racist caricatures. A large body of research has shown that Native-themed mascots perpetuate stereotypes and have negative effects on Native youth and how they view themselves and their communities. The American Psychological Association called for the retirement of all Native-themed mascots in 2005.

Background

With the growth of professional sports leagues in the United States in the early 20th century, it became common for teams to name themselves after Native peoples and to adopt Native-themed mascots and logos. A significant number of those names and images remain in use today. These teams and some of their fans have claimed that their Native themes are meant to honour Native peoples, but many Native peoples strongly disagree. They argue that Native-themed mascots and logos are a harmful relic of the country's long history of racism and discrimination against Native peoples. In the 1960s Native activists began a movement to end the use of Native-names, mascots, and logos in American sports. The movement has achieved many successes, and its efforts continue today.

Activism and Progress

In 1968 the National Congress of American Indians (NCAI) began a campaign against the use of Native stereotypes in popular culture, including sports. Other Native rights groups—including the American Indian Movement (AIM)—also took up the cause. For many years the NCAI focused mainly on lobbying professional sports teams to discontinue their use of Native-themed names and symbols. Activists held protests, filed lawsuits, and pressured corporations to end their support of teams with offensive names and symbols. However, strong resistance from team owners and fans delayed change for decades.

Meanwhile, schools at the university and lower levels made progress in changing Native-themed team names and mascots. The University of Oklahoma retired its Native mascot, known as "Little Red," in 1970. Within the next few years Stanford University and Dartmouth College dropped the nickname Indians and their Native mascots. These schools set an example that many other universities, colleges, and high schools followed over the decades to come. In 2005 the National Collegiate Athletic Association banned teams that use Native-themed names, logos, and mascots from its championship tournaments.

State governments also took action to curb the use of Native mascots and logos. By 2022 more than 20 states had taken steps to address the use of Native-themed mascots in public high schools and elementary schools. In 2019 Maine became the first state to pass a full ban on the use of Native mascots in public schools. In 2023 New York state ruled that schools that did not retire their Native mascots by 2025 risked losing state funding.

Continuing pressure finally helped bring about progress in professional sports beginning in the 2010s. One major success came in Cleveland. The city's Major League Baseball (MLB) team was named the Cleveland Indians in 1915, and in the 1940s it adopted a logo known as Chief Wahoo. The logo was a red-faced cartoon figure that was widely criticized as a racist caricature of a Native man. Protests against Chief Wahoo began in the 1970s, but it was not until the 2010s that the team began phasing out the logo. It was officially retired in 2018. Before the 2022 season the team changed its name to the Cleveland Guardians.

Another long-standing target of Native activists was the National Football League (NFL) team from Washington, D.C. Since 1933 the team had been playing as the Redskins, a word generally ranked among the worst racial slurs that could be used against Native people. The team logo featured a profile of a Native man with feathers in his hair. Activists, including Suzan Shown Harjo, filed a lawsuit against the team in 1992, but for almost three decades the team's owners refused to change the name. In 2020, under pressure from corporate sponsors, the owners finally agreed to drop the offensive term. The club played as the Washington Football Team during the 2020 and 2021 seasons before adopting the name Commanders in 2022.

Ongoing Efforts

The NCAI and other groups continue to pressure other professional teams to change their names, logos, and mascots. For example, the logo of the Atlanta Braves MLB team is a tomahawk, an ax historically used as a weapon by some Native Americans. Fans of the team perform what they call the "tomahawk chop"—an arm movement that is accompanied by a mock "war chant." Both the team and the MLB have endorsed the continuation of the practice. Other teams have not moved to change their names but have taken small steps to try to be more sensitive to Native peoples. For instance, the Kansas City Chiefs of the NFL and the Chicago Blackhawks of the National Hockey League no longer allow fans to wear Native headdresses to games. The Chiefs also banned face paint that references Native people or culture.

Are Team Names and Mascots that Use Cultural Appropriation Acceptable?

Activists continue their work at the local level as well. Although professional teams have received the most attention, owing to their massive audiences and extensive media reach, most Native-themed names and mascots are used in schools. The NCAI keeps a database of elementary, middle, and high schools with teams that have Native-themed mascots. In 2023 the database still included some 1,900 schools—mostly high schools—throughout the United States.

The impact that Native-themed mascots and stereotypes have had on the Native population is explored in the documentary *Imagining the Indian: The Fight Against Native American Mascoting* (2021).

VIEWPOINT 4

> *"Implicit bias can influence decisions ranging from hiring practices to jury preferences and criminal sentencing. And it's all the more pernicious because the people making these biased decisions are unlikely to be aware that they're doing so."*

Native American Mascots Reinforce Negative Stereotypes

Justin Angle

Justin Angle writes that despite the notion that team names and mascots featuring Native American tropes are harmless, conversely, they can have negative psychological effects. Even superficial exposure to these names and images can reinforce negative stereotypes, he contends. In conducting research in cities with Indigenous team names, Angle found that the more offensive the mascot was, the more ordinary citizens were likely to associate negative connotations with Indigenous people. Justin Angle is a professor of marketing at the University of Montana. His academic research focuses on how people express their identities through their consumption behaviors. He is also the creator and host of the Edward R. Murrow Award-winning podcast "Fireline."

"New research shows how Native American mascots reinforce stereotypes," by Justin Angle, The Conversation, September 13, 2016. https://theconversation.com/new-research-shows-how-native-american-mascots-reinforce-stereotypes-63861. Licensed CC BY-ND 4.0 International.

Are Team Names and Mascots that Use Cultural Appropriation Acceptable?

As you read, consider the following questions:

1. According to Angle, how do Indigenous team names foster implicit bias against Indigenous people?
2. What argument do defenders of Native American team names use to justify their endurance?
3. How were liberal participants in Angle's study especially sensitive to the influence of Indigenous team names?

For years, many have said that sports teams with Native American mascots – the Cleveland Indians, Chicago Blackhawks and Florida State Seminoles, to name a few – perpetuate stereotypes against Native people. Others have argued that these mascots are harmless; if anything, they symbolize reverence and respect, while honoring the history of Native Americans.

At the epicenter of the debate have been the Washington Redskins, a football team worth nearly US$3 billion. But as the Redskins kicked off their season on Sept. 12, there was hardly a mention of the name controversy that has, in recent years, elicited boycotts, lawsuits and protests.

Perhaps it's due to the *Washington Post* survey from last spring finding that 90 percent of the Native Americans polled weren't offended by the Redskins name. Since then, defenders of the name – including team owner Daniel Snyder – have considered the controversy over and done with. The "sticks and stones" argument suggested by the poll makes complete sense from a self-preservation standpoint; after all, Native Americans have had to persevere through worse offenses than mascots.

But that stance ignores the dangerous possibility that such ethnic names and imagery affect how *other people* view Native Americans – possibly in subtle and damaging ways.

Our research has shown that incidental exposure to Native American sports mascots can reinforce stereotypes in people. Perhaps more disturbingly, people aren't even aware that this subtle reinforcement is taking place.

How a Name Strengthens a Bias

In our lab, we showed participants an unfamiliar mascot; some were shown a Native American image, while others were shown an image of an animal. We then measured how strongly all participants associated Native Americans with "warlike," a stereotype leveraged by many sports teams that use Native mascots ("Braves," "Warriors"). When asked directly, participants, regardless of the mascot they saw, reported no differences in how warlike they thought Native Americans were.

But when participants completed an indirect – or implicit – stereotype measure, those who'd viewed the Native American mascot were more likely to associate warlike qualities with Native Americans.

This difference in results represents something called implicit bias, which often takes place when asking people about socially sensitive subjects such as race or gender. Our participants were either unwilling to admit or unaware of the mascot's influence on their views of Native Americans; their bias was implicit, either hidden or incognizant.

Implicit bias can influence decisions ranging from hiring practices to jury preferences and criminal sentencing. And it's all the more pernicious because the people making these biased decisions are unlikely to be aware that they're doing so.

Interestingly, the liberal participants in our studies were more affected by Native American mascots than were their conservative peers.

Because liberals often think of themselves as being less susceptible to racial bias, this might seem counterintuitive. But liberals also have been shown to have more malleable worldviews and be more open to new information. And in our study, we found a stereotypical mascot could significantly degrade liberals' attitudes toward Native Americans.

Some Mascots More Damaging than Others

These lab results prompted us to try to replicate our findings in a real world setting. If the media market you live in determines how often you're exposed to a Native American sports mascot, we would expect to see differences in attitudes toward Native Americans between people who live in cities with Native American-themed sports franchises and people who don't. Indeed, our results showed that people living in cities with Native American mascots were more likely to think of Native Americans as warlike.

We decided to focus on the Cleveland and Atlanta media markets because the Native American mascots of their baseball teams – the Indians and the Braves – were considered the most and least offensive examples, respectively, according to a pre-experiment survey. (Detroit, home of the Tigers, and Miami, which houses the Marlins, were used as control cities.)

Using the same implicit measures as our earlier study, residents of Cleveland were more likely to associate Native Americans with warlike traits than residents of Atlanta, Detroit and Miami.

In other words, the more offensive the mascot, the greater the effect.

And just like in our lab, liberal participants were particularly sensitive to the influence of the Native American mascot. The study represents perhaps the first real-world demonstration of the adverse effects of incidental exposure to Native American sports mascots in the general population.

The Perils of Stereotypes

Some might wonder what the problem is with being seen as warlike. After all, isn't that associated with bravery and toughness?

But studies have shown how stereotypes of any kind – even positive ones – carry consequences. They can lead to performance anxiety, as Sapna Cheryan and her colleagues found when looking at stereotypes concerning Asian Americans' math ability. Subsequent studies have shown how experiencing a positive stereotype can make people expect future prejudicial treatment.

Despite these findings, defenders of Native American mascots continue to argue that the mascots honor Native Americans and improve perceptions of Native people.

Furthermore, stereotypical representations of minority groups aren't just relegated to Native American team mascots.

Many prominent brands, such as Aunt Jemimah, Uncle Ben's and Land-O-Lakes Butter, actively promote certain stereotypes. And as our study showed, these representations can change how we think about the actual members of those groups – often without us even knowing it.

So when it comes to the Washington Redskins – despite the results of the spring poll – the evidence is clear: The presence of the name subconsciously causes people to stereotype Native Americans. Even President Obama has weighed in, recommending a new name.

He's right. It's high time for change.

VIEWPOINT 5

> "To mana-munch a person's spirit through disparaging, racist and misappropriated mascots and branding is nothing short of dehumanizing the legacy of the living, their ancestors and those yet to be born."

Team Names Should Foster Positive Energy, Not Negative Racist Energy
Paul Whitinui

Paul Whitinui writes from an Indigenous perspective about the harm done by negative portrayals of Native peoples through disparaging mascots. Whitinui specifically focuses on the effect of these mascots on Indigenous people. He discusses the concept of mana, or spiritual energy, suggesting that this energy is sapped by demeaning portrayals, such as those presented by racist team names and mascots. Whitinui believes it is much better to focus on the positive regarding mascots and enhance the mana of all peoples rather than diminishing it. Paul Whitinui is an Indigenous Māori scholar from Aotearoa, New Zealand. He is a professor in the faculty of education at the School of Exercise Science, Physical and Health Education at the University of Victoria in British Columbia, Canada.

"Washington Redskins finally agree: Dismantling racist team mascots is long overdue," by Paul Whitinui, The Conversation, July 14, 2020. https://theconversation.com/washington-redskins-finally-agree-dismantling-racist-team-mascots-is-long-overdue-142618. Licensed CC BY-ND 4.0 International.

Cultural Appropriation

As you read, consider the following questions:

1. According to Whitinui, how did the killing of George Floyd finally galvanize public opinion against Indigenous mascots?
2. According to Whitinui, what is the origin of the term "mascot"?
3. Why does Whitinui believe that polls taken about the use of Indigenous mascots are not reliable?

The Washington Redskins, facing increased public and financial pressure, have finally announced they will change their team nickname. This decision puts an end to almost 30 years of active protest and litigation against the National Football League franchise.

Following the brutal killing of George Floyd by police in Minneapolis on May 25, the Black Lives Matter movement effectively mobilized the world to stand united against racialized acts of violence.

The idea of sports teams changing their racist logos, names or brands became part of the campaign against systemic racism, though it is not new. Since 1969, 14 North American sports teams have removed their names or logos that were outwardly racist towards First Nations and Native Americans.

The Redskins

In 2014, in the Amanda Blackhorse vs. Pro Football Inc. case, the United States Patent and Trademark Office ruled that the Washington NFL team's name was disparaging to Indigenous Peoples.

At the time, Amanda Blackhorse was interviewed by journalist Steve Paikin on *The Agenda*. She said the Washington Redskins mascot name is an outwardly racist, offensive and disparaging slur.

Four years later, the Supreme Court ruled in favour of allowing the team to use the name. Blackhorse told *USA Today*:

> We said the term 'Redskins' is disparaging and the courts agreed with us … it's just that now the Supreme Court says it's OK to register a disparaging term.

The name reinforces racist stereotypes targeting Navajo Indians as "Redskins."

The Redskin controversy dates back to 1775 when a document called the Phips Proclamation named after Spencer Phips, a British politician and then Lieutenant Governor of the Massachusetts Bay Province, placed a bounty on the heads of Penobscot Indians, a tribe now based in Maine. A "Redskin" was said to be a scalped head of a Native American, sold, like a pelt, for cash.

Similarly, up until 2019, the Cleveland Indians major league baseball team used a cartoon character called Chief Wahoo. Wahoo was depicted as a Redskin, who is often ridiculed in ways that are offensive to Native Americans.

The Problem with Opinion Polls

A 2019 poll conducted by Angus Reid said that more than half of Canadians believe sports franchises that use Indigenous naming and imagery should not have to change.

However, the problem with these polls is the silencing of Indigenous voices. It's like taking a general survey about the correct pronunciation of an Indigenous place name in Cree when all Canadians predominantly speak English and French. It makes no sense. What we need are fluent Cree speakers who can help us learn the correct pronunciation.

The word mascot originates from the French, *mascotte*, which means my lucky charm. Mascot also has several derivatives, including *maso*, meaning witch or sorceress; *mascoto*, meaning spell or bewitchment. It has been associated with inanimate objects that were commonly seen as either a lock of hair, a figurehead on a sailing ship or good luck animals used to represent one's group identity.

In modern sport, mascots are used for good luck. But they are also used to build merchandising revenue, meet monetary targets and increase the fan base. Team mascots often take the form of a logo, person, live animal, a costumed character or other inanimate objects.

But what happens when team mascots are used to misrepresent or misappropriate groups of people who then feel constantly ridiculed, violated and delegitimized as human beings because of the way team mascots are paraded, adorned and validated?

This might include outwardly racist slurs, misappropriation of images related to First Nations/Native Americans, a public mocking of First Nations/Native Americans regalia, or other misconstrued terms to further dehumanize a group of people.

How a School District Got Rid of Offensive Mascots

Four schools in the Houston Independent School District (HISD) debuted new mascots on Tuesday, replacing previous ones that had sparked complaints of being offensive to Native American groups.

The school athletic teams will be called the Lamar High School Texans, Hamilton Middle School Huskies, Westbury High School Huskies and Welch Middle School Wolf Pack, replacing mascot names Redskins, Indians, Rebels and Warriors, respectively.

HISD, one of the largest school districts in the United States, made the decision to change the mascot names last year at a school board meeting after several Native Americans said the references were racially and culturally insensitive.

Schools across the country have been re-examining team names and mascots amid ongoing controversy surrounding those of professional sports teams, particularly the National Football League's Washington Redskins.

The Oneida tribe in New York State is behind a campaign that wants the NFL to force the Redskins franchise to change its team name — which many Native Americans consider a racial slur — and mascot.

[...]

The tribe has also been strongly opposed to the use of the name "redskins" in schools, and has followed the HISD mascot controversy closely.

> According to the Houston Chronicle, the school district will spend nearly $50,000 on new uniforms for fall sports, and additional costs are expected for spring uniforms and the replacement of old mascot names and images on various facilities.
>
> Houston is not the only city facing issues over school mascots. California's Coachella Valley High School drew fierce criticism from the Arab-American community in November over its longstanding team name, Coachella Valley Arabs, and mascot, an angry-looking Arab man. While the school district expressed willingness to work with Arab-American groups to reach an amicable solution to the controversy, the name and mascot remain.
>
> Following a series of similar controversies, Wisconsin Gov. Scott Walker signed a law last year making it tougher to force schools to change their mascots. The new law requires at least 10 percent of a school district's membership to sign a complaint to be reviewed by the state's Department of Public Instruction before a mascot change can be considered.
>
> The law also places the burden to prove that a team name or mascot promotes discrimination on those who file the complaint.
>
> "Houston school district abandons mascots offensive to Native Americans," by César Albarrán-Torres and Liam Burke, Al Jazeera Media Network, November 3, 2022.

Resistance to Change

The National Congress of Indians (NCAI) published a database in 2013 which found more than 2,000 secondary schools with mascots that reference Native American culture, compared to around 3,000 from 50 years ago. Since the 1960s, the NCAI has been a powerful advocate for spearheading laws and regulations that Native logos need to end everywhere.

Racially constructed names pertaining to the Braves, Chiefs, Redskins, Indians, Blackhawks and Seminoles remain a point of contention among many Indigenous Peoples living in Canada.

Earlier this year, the Edmonton Eskimos of the Canadian Football League decided against changing their name — but then said in July it was reassessing the name once again. The team said its original decision was based on the premise that it had consulted with the Inuit community who stand by the name "Eskimos."

But the Inuit are not Eskimos, and according to fluent speaking Inuit members, Eskimos means "meat eater," not Inuit.

But elsewhere, other teams are changing racist names. The amateur Saanich Junior B "Braves" hockey team on Vancouver Island recently decided to change its name out of respect for First Nations Peoples.

Mana-Munching Is Not Our Way

Article 31 of the UN Declaration on the Rights of Indigenous Peoples states that Indigenous Peoples have the right to maintain, control, protect and develop their cultural heritage, traditional knowledge and traditional cultural expressions.

Anything less diminishes the *mana* of a people.

Mana is a word well known and used among many Indigenous Peoples of the Pacific and North America. In Hawaii and New Zealand, for example, *mana* means the spiritual energy, healing power or essence a person carries with them from one generation to the next. To disrespect, demean or desecrate a person's mana in any way is to diminish who they are, and in doing so to dishonour all they are and can be – this is not our way.

A more respectful approach to enhancing the mana of a person, as articulated by performer and researcher Te Ahukaramū Charles Royal, is the idea that we should all work together to hold each other up so that a person can realize their full potential.

To *mana-munch* a person's spirit through disparaging, racist and misappropriated mascots and branding is nothing short of dehumanizing the legacy of the living, their ancestors and those yet to be born. It is an intergenerational practice Indigenous Peoples know only too well and is an integral part of our identity and who we are as human beings.

Mascots that enhance the mana of all people rather than diminish them is the preferred teaching because it impacts every aspect of our society or world. In this era of Truth and

Reconciliation, we can work together to reconcile our differences, repair the past and heal. Team mascots have a role and responsibility to respect the living and build positive relationships that can enhance the spirit of sports we all love and enjoy.

Cultural Appropriation

Periodical and Internet Sources Bibliography

The following articles have been selected to supplement the diverse views presented in this chapter.

"More than Mascots: It's Time to End Cultural Appropriation of Native Americans in Sports," Nielsen, May 2021. https://www.nielsen.com/insights/2021/more-than-mascots-its-time-to-end-cultural-appropriation-of-native-americans-in-sports/.

"Pennsylvania Still Has 66 Racist Public School Mascots," Pennsylvania Youth Congress, July 3, 2020. https://payouthcongress.org/2020/07/03/racistmascotsinpa/.

Alyssa Burr, "Dozens of Michigan Schools Still Use Native American Slurs, Imagery," *MLive*, October 17, 2021. https://www.mlive.com/public-interest/2021/10/dozens-of-michigan-schools-still-use-native-american-slurs-imagery.html?outputType=amp.

Brittany L. Cerny, "Native American Mascots in Sports Teams: Cultural Appropriation or a Symbol of Honor?," PowWows.com, February 6, 2023. https://www.powwows.com/native-american-mascots-in-sports-teams-cultural-appropriation-or-a-symbol-of-honor/.

Marc Chalufour, "Should Sports Teams Change Their Native-Inspired Names?," *Bostonia*, October 29, 2021. https://www.bu.edu/articles/2021/should-sports-teams-change-their-native-inspired-names/.

WaziHanska Cook, "It's Past Time to Eliminate Racist Native Mascots," Teach for America, September 3, 2020. https://www.teachforamerica.org/one-day/top-issues/its-past-time-to-eliminate-racist-native-mascots.

Kim Eckart, "Bias Against Native Americans Spikes When Mascots Are Removed," UWNews, December 16, 2021. https://www.washington.edu/news/2021/12/16/bias-against-native-americans-spikes-when-mascots-are-removed/.

Mike Freeman, "Opinion: New Nielsen Poll Offers Hope that We'll 'See the End of Native Mascots," *USA Today*, May 16, 2021. https://www.usatoday.com/story/sports/columnist/mike-freeman/2021/05/16/native-american-mascots-washington-football-cleveland/5107668001/.

Dana Hunsinger Benbow, "Notre Dame Defends Leprechaun Mascot, Ranked College Football's 4th-Most Offensive in Study," *IndyStar*, August 23, 2021. https://www.indystar.com/story/sports/college/2021/08/23/notre-dame-defends-fighting-irish-leprechaun-mascot-ranked-offensive/8249420002/.

Craig Idlebrook, "Bitter Debates, Voter Backlash Follow Efforts to Rename Sports Teams," *Hill Country Observer*, June 2021. https://www.hillcountryobserver.com/2021news/June2021Culture%20clash.htm.

Kate Lisa, "N.Y. State Budget Won't Include Funding for School Indigenous Mascot Ban," Spectrum News 1, April 24, 2023. https://spectrumlocalnews.com/nys/central-ny/politics/2023/04/24/state-budget-won-t-include-funding-for-school-indigenous-mascot-ban.

Calum Trenaman, "Global Sport's Problem with the Appropriation of Indigenous Culture," CNN, January 18, 2021. https://www.cnn.com/2021/01/18/sport/indigenous-culture-in-global-sport-cmd-spt-intl/index.html.

For Further Discussion

Chapter 1
1. After reading the viewpoints in this chapter, how would you define "cultural appropriation"?
2. Viewpoints such as those by Kenan Malik, Andy Pratt, and Steve Patterson are critical of cultural appropriation accusations, arguing that they are often unhelpful and divisive. Do you agree or disagree? Explain your reasoning.
3. Some authors in this chapter insist that cultural appropriation is indefensible. Can you think of some circumstances in which it may be defensible to use cultural appropriation?

Chapter 2
1. After reading the viewpoints in this chapter, do you feel that cultural appropriation is a major issue in the music industry? Why or why not?
2. Based on what you've read in these viewpoints, are there some instances of cultural appropriation in music that are acceptable? Explain your reasoning.
3. After reading the viewpoints in this chapter, why do you believe cultural appropriation is so prevalent in music?

Chapter 3
1. After reading the viewpoints in this chapter, do you believe whitewashing is still a major problem in cinema?
2. After reading the viewpoint by Gene Demby and Rachel Martin, why do you believe the practice of blackface is so ingrained and difficult to eliminate?
3. After reading the viewpoint by Bob Mondello, what is your opinion on cross-cultural or color-blind casting? Explain your reasoning.

Chapter 4

1. After reading the viewpoints in this chapter, do you believe there are some Indigenous mascots that are acceptable, or should all of them be eliminated? Explain your reasoning.
2. After reading the viewpoints by Sam Hitchmough, Justin Angle, and Paul Whitinui, why do you believe it has taken so long to eliminate the truly offensive mascots?
3. Based on what you've read in the viewpoints in this chapter, why have Indigenous mascots at high schools and other local schools persisted into the 21st century when others, such as NFL, MLB, and college mascots, have been changed or eliminated?

Organizations to Contact

The editors have compiled the following list of organizations concerned with the issues debated in this book. The descriptions are derived from materials provided by the organizations. All have publications or information available for interested readers. The list was compiled on the date of publication of the present volume; the information provided here may change. Be aware that many organizations take several weeks or longer to respond to inquiries, so allow as much time as possible.

American Civil Liberties Union (ACLU)
125 Broad Street
New York, NY 10004-2400
(212) 549-2500
website: www.aclu.org

The ACLU considers itself to be the nation's guardian of liberty, working in courts, legislatures, and communities to defend and preserve the individual rights and liberties that the Constitution and the laws of the United States guarantee. Among the issues it focuses on are human rights, racial equality, and women's rights.

American Enterprise Institute (AEI)
1789 Massachusetts Avenue, NW
Washington, DC 20036
(202) 862-5800
email: tyler.castle@aei.org
website: www.aei.org

The American Enterprise Institute is a conservative public policy think tank that sponsors original research on the world economy, U.S. foreign policy and international security, and domestic political and social issues. AEI is dedicated to defending human dignity, expanding human potential, and building a freer and safer world. Its scholars and staff advance ideas rooted in their belief in democracy and free enterprise.

Cato Institute
1000 Massachusetts Avenue NW
Washington, DC 20001
(202) 842-0200
website: www.cato.org

The Cato Institute is a libertarian public policy research organization and think tank dedicated to the principles of individual liberty, limited government, free markets, and peace. Its scholars and analysts conduct independent research on a wide range of policy issues.

Center for American Progress (CAP)
1333 H Street NW, 10th Floor
Washington, DC 20005
(202) 682-1611
website: www.americanprogress.org

The Center for American Progress is a public policy research and advocacy organization that presents a liberal viewpoint on economic and social issues. Its website includes a range of articles on various social issues.

Greenheart International
742 N. LaSalle Drive, Suite 300
Chicago, IL 60654
(866) 224-0061
website: https://greenheart.org

Since 1985, Greenheart International has been a catalyst for global transformation through the facilitation of cultural exchange programs, personal development opportunities, volunteer service initiatives, and environmental advocacy projects. Its mission of connecting people and planet to create global leaders drives all that it does in Greenheart Travel and Greenheart Exchange. Greenheart's two branches focus on cultural exchange—both inbound to the U.S. with Greenheart Exchange and outbound from the U.S. with Greenheart Travel.

The Indian Law Resource Center

602 North Ewing Street
Helena, MT 59601
(406) 449-2006
email: mt@indianlaw.org
website: https://indianlaw.org

The Indian Law Resource Center provides legal assistance to Indigenous peoples of the Americas to combat racism and oppression, to protect their lands and environment, to protect their cultures and ways of life, to achieve sustainable economic development and genuine self-government, and to realize their other human rights. The Resource Center seeks to overcome the grave problems that threaten Native peoples by advancing the rule of law, establishing national and international legal standards that preserve their human rights and dignity, and challenging the governments of the world to accord justice and equality before the law to all Indigenous peoples of the Americas.

International Work Group for Indigenous Affairs (IWGIA)

Prinsessegade 29 B, 3rd floor
DK 1422
Copenhagen, Denmark
(+45) 53 73 28 30
email: iwgia@iwgia.org
website: www.iwgia.org/en

IWGIA is a global human rights organization dedicated to promoting and defending Indigenous peoples' rights. IWGIA was founded in 1968 by anthropologists alarmed about the ongoing genocide of Indigenous peoples taking place in the Amazon.

National Association for the Advancement of Colored People (NAACP)

4805 Mt. Hope Drive
Baltimore, MD 21215
(410) 580-5777
email: washingtonbureau@naacpnet.org
website: https://naacp.org

Founded in 1909, the NAACP is an interracial American organization that works for the abolition of segregation and discrimination in housing, education, employment, voting, and transportation. It opposes racism and strives to ensure that Black Americans have their constitutional rights. The NAACP engages in grassroots activism for civil rights and social justice. It advocates, agitates, and litigates for the civil rights due to Black America.

National Congress of American Indians (NCAI)

1516 P Street NW
Washington, DC 20005
(202) 466-7767
email: NCAIPress@ncai.org.
website: www.ncai.org

Founded in 1944, the National Congress of American Indians (NCAI) is the oldest, largest, and most representative American Indian and Alaska Native organization serving the broad interests of tribal governments and communities. NCAI, a non-profit organization, advocates for a bright future for generations to come by taking the lead to gain consensus on a constructive and promising vision for Indian Country. The organization's policy issues and initiatives are driven by the consensus of its diverse membership, which consists of American Indian and Alaska Native tribal governments, tribal citizens, individuals, and Native and non-Native organizations.

Teach For America

315 West 36th Street, Eighth Floor
New York, NY 10018
(212) 279-2080
website: www.teachforamerica.org

Teach For America is a leadership development organization for those who want to co-create a more just world alongside young people in their communities. They are a network of nearly 70,000 leaders who started in the classroom and remain in lifelong pursuit of the vision that one day, all children will have the opportunity to attain an excellent education.

U.S. Commission on Civil Rights (USCCR)

1331 Pennsylvania Avenue NW, Suite 1150
Washington, DC 20425
(202) 376-7700
website: www.usccr.gov

Established as an independent, bipartisan, fact-finding government agency, the USCCR's mission is to inform the development of national civil rights policy and enhance enforcement of federal civil rights laws. It pursues this mission by studying alleged deprivations of voting rights and alleged discrimination based on race, color, religion, sex, age, disability, or national origin, or in the administration of justice. It plays a vital role in advancing civil rights through objective and comprehensive investigation, research, and analysis on issues of fundamental concern to the federal government and the public. its journal, *Civil Rights*, along with other relevant publications, is available on its website.

Bibliography of Books

Katharine Bausc. *He Thinks He's Down: White Appropriations of Black Masculinities in the Civil Rights Era.* Vancouver, BC: UBC Press, 2020.

Enrico Bonadio and Chen Wei Zhu, eds. *Music Borrowing and Copyright Law: A Genre-by-Genre Analysis.* Oxford, UK: Hart Publishing, 2023.

John Borrows and Kent McNeil, eds. *Voicing Identity: Cultural Appropriation and Indigenous Issues.* Toronto, ON: University of Toronto Press, 2022.

Elizabeth M. Bucar. *Stealing My Religion: Not Just Any Cultural Appropriation.* Cambridge, MA: Harvard University Press, 2022.

Lisa A. Crayton, *Everything You Need to Know About Cultural Appropriation.* New York, NY: Rosen Publishing, 2019.

Jonita Davis. *Questioning Cultural Appropriation.* New York, NY: Enslow Publishing, 2018.

Philip Joseph Deloria. *Playing Indian.* New Haven, CT: Yale University Press, 2022.

M. M. Eboch, ed. *Cultural Appropriation.* New York, NY: Greenhaven Publishing, 2020.

Heather C. Hudak. *Cultural Appropriation.* Collingwood, ON: Coast2Coast, Canada, 2020.

Lauren Michele Jackson. *White Negroes: When Cornrows Were in Vogue…and Other Thoughts on Cultural Appropriation.* Boston, MA: Beacon Press, 2019.

Tabea Jerrentrup. *A Twisted Style: The Culture of Dreadlocks in "Western" Societies.* New York, NY: Berghahn Books, 2021.

Yuniya Kawamura and Jung-Whan Marc De Jong. *Cultural Appropriation in Fashion and Entertainment.* London, UK: Bloomsbury Visual Arts, 2022.

Matthias Krings. *African Appropriations: Cultural Difference, Mimesis, and Media.* Bloomington, IN: Indiana University Press, 2015.

Jamil Mustafa. *The Blaxploitation Horror Film: Adaptation, Appropriation and the Gothic.* Cardiff, UK: University of Wales Press, 2023.

Martin Puchner. *Culture: The Story of Us, from Cave Art to K-Pop.* New York, NY: W.W. Norton, 2023.

James O. Young and Conrad G. Brunk. *The Ethics of Cultural Appropriation.* Chichester, UK: Wiley-Blackwell, 2012.

Bruce H. Ziff and Pratima V. Rao. *Borrowed Power: Essays on Cultural Appropriation.* New Brunswick, NJ: Rutgers University Press, 1997.

Index

A

Affleck, Ben, 101
Armstrong, Louis, 88
Asians/Asian culture
   cultural appropriation of, 16, 95, 96, 99–100, 108, 109, 123
   whitewashing and, 109
Atlanta Braves, 16, 141, 146, 151
Azalea, Iggy, 20–21, 72, 79, 81, 84

B

Beastie Boys, 65–66
Berry, Chuck, 73
Beyonce, 29, 33, 81, 82–83
Bieber, Justin, 29, 33, 35, 36, 79
Birth of a Nation, 101, 108, 109–110
Black culture, appropriation of, 22, 59, 95
   hairstyles, 26–27, 29, 31, 33, 44–48, 55, 58
   music, 16, 20, 21, 58, 65, 69, 70–72, 73, 75–80, 86–90
blackface, 75, 78, 80, 94, 95, 96, 101, 108, 109, 113–118, 136
blackfishing, 21
Black Panther, 35, 103–107
blues music, 20, 42, 58, 70, 88
Bollywood, 29, 33, 83, 84
Boseman, Chadwick, 105

Breakfast at Tiffany's, 16, 99–100, 109
Bridgerton, 124–125

C

Cardi B, 79
censorship, 14, 17, 43, 99–100
Cher, 68, 71
Chicago Blackhawks, 140, 146, 149
Clapton, Eric, 20, 66
Cleveland Indians, 26, 133, 134, 138, 139, 145–146, 149, 151, 155
Coachella festival, 26
Coldplay, 81, 82–83
colonialism, 30, 37, 51, 70, 104, 107, 140
critical thinking, 11–13
cultural appreciation, 20, 21, 22, 25, 35–39, 40, 66, 79
cultural appropriation
   avoiding, 52–53, 68, 74
   defense of, 54–59
   defining, 22–27, 29, 32, 37, 50, 69, 79
   disrespect and, 41–42, 52
   effects/harm of, 16, 22, 23–25, 27, 51, 73, 80, 144, 148–152, 153–159
   insult or homage?, 19–60
   "policing" of, 15, 28, 33–34

using it for personal gain, 19–21, 22, 25–27, 37, 47, 49, 51, 72, 75, 77
cultural exchange, 14, 36, 38, 40, 42, 43, 47, 52, 53, 58, 60–61, 79–80
culture
   argument against importance of all aspects, 56–57, 59–60
   defined, 25, 29–30
   exploiting minority culture, 22, 44–48, 49, 69–70, 75, 76, 77–78
   "ownership" of, 31, 54, 55
   respecting/honoring, 15, 20, 40, 42, 70
Cyrus, Miley, 68, 71–72, 80, 84

D

Depp, Johnny, 101
Die Antwoord, 75–80
Disney, Walt, 94–95
diversity, 39, 52, 103, 104, 106, 112, 124
dreadlocks, 26–27, 29, 31, 33, 36, 55

E

Elba, Idris, 123, 125

F

fashion industry, 36, 38, 43, 51
film industry, 16, 94–125
   colorblind and cross-cultural casting, 111, 119–125

Florida State Seminoles, 131, 142, 149

G

gatekeeping, 28, 29, 31, 33–34
Gershwin, George, 86–90
Grande, Ariana, 79
group identity, 57–58, 155

H

Halloween costumes, 24, 29, 31–32, 51–52
Hamilton, 111, 119, 121, 124
headdresses, Native American, 24, 26, 31, 32, 52, 135, 136, 140, 146
Hepburn, Audrey, 99, 100
hijabs, 40–43
hip-hop/rap, 59, 65–66, 75–80, 84, 121
Huerta, Tenoch, 103, 105, 106, 107

I

identity politics, 16, 30
Indian/Southesast Asian culture, appropriation of, 15, 29, 33, 36, 38, 70, 82–83
Indigenous cultures, appropriation of, 36, 37–38, 46
   harm to women and, 23–25, 32
   Native Americans/First Nations, 16, 22, 26, 29, 31–32, 38, 52, 58, 71, 95, 101–102, 118, 129–159
   for sports teams, 16, 26, 129–131, 132–137, 138–142, 143–147, 148–152, 153–159

Index

intellectual property rights, 53, 60

J

jazz, 86–90
Jenner, Kendall, 36
Jenner, Kylie, 29, 47
Johansson, Scarlett, 109, 111
Johnson, James P., 88, 89
Johnson, Robert, 20
Jolson, Al, 113, 115
Jones, James Earl, 122
Joplin, Janice, 16
Jordan, Michael B., 35, 38, 39

K

Kansas City Chiefs, 132, 133, 134–135, 141, 146
Kardashian, Kim, 21, 38, 39
Kardashian/Jenner family, 21, 29, 35, 36, 38, 39

L

Latin American culture
  appropriation of, 70
  whitewashing and, 109, 110–112
Led Zeppelin, 71
LGBTQ+ culture, appropriation of, 22, 25, 70
Little Richard, 73

M

Madonna, 25, 68, 70, 81, 84
Marley, Bob, 20
Mars, Bruno, 79–90

McGill University, 129–130, 138, 142
Mexican culture, 103–107
  appropriation of, 36, 38
Mickey Mouse, 94–95, 113, 115, 117
Miranda, Lin-Manuel, 111, 121
music industry, 16, 20, 42, 45, 46–47, 60, 65–90

N

Native Americans/First Nations, and cultural appropriation, 16, 22, 26, 29, 31–32, 38, 52, 58, 71, 95, 101–102, 118, 129–159
Nike, 43

O

opposing viewpoints, importance of, 11–13
#OscarsSoWhite, 96, 98–99, 112

P

Patel, Dev, 120, 124, 125
Post Malone, 79
Presley, Elvis, 66, 69, 73

R

racism, 15, 16, 20, 21, 26–27, 30–31, 56, 60, 74, 77, 94–95, 98–100, 107, 112, 118, 136, 139–140, 142, 144, 146, 153, 154, 156
reading comprehension, 12–13
reggae, 20, 71

"Rhapsody in Blue," 86–90
rock and roll, 16, 42, 58, 69, 70–71, 73
Rolling Stones, 66, 70
Rooney, Mickey, 16, 99–100, 109
Rubin, Rick, 65
Rushdie, Salman, 33

S

Seinfeld, 19–20
Shriver, Lionel, 14–15, 16, 17
Simmons, Russell, 65
skin, darkening, 15, 21, 78
Skrein, Ed, 108, 109, 112
Smith, Bessie, 88–89
Smith, Willie "The Lion," 88
social media, 116–117, 120
South Africa, 75–80
sports teams and cultural appropriation, 16, 26, 118, 129–159
  mascots, 133–135, 136, 141, 144–145, 147, 148–152, 153–159
Stefani, Gwen, 84
stereotypes, 24, 26, 28, 31, 32, 52, 133, 136, 141
Swinton, Tilda, 108, 112

T

Thornton, Big Mama, 16
Till, Emmett, 41–42
"tomahawk chop," 16, 118, 134, 135, 136, 146
trap music, 72

V

Vanilla Ice, 66
"Vogue," 25, 70

W

Wakanda Forever, 103–107
Washington Redskins, 16, 132, 133, 138, 139, 146, 149, 152, 154–155
Waters, Muddy, 20, 70
Wayne, John, 109, 110, 123
Whiteman, Paul, 87, 89–90
whitewashing in film industry, 96, 97–102, 108–112

Y

yoga, 15, 29, 31

Index

Cultural Appropriation